Comments From Fellow R

We ordered your sleep coach system about two weeks ago and things are going so well for us. Since then he has been falling asleep on his own at six forty five with no crying. What a breakthrough for us! He is sleeping twelve hours straight now.

My husband and I just want to thank you so much for helping us. We are getting more sleep, our relationship is so much better with each other and with him. We were laughing the other night because after Josh went to bed we were able to watch a movie together...it was kind of like a date even though we were on our couch! I never realized before how having a child can negatively affect a marriage and I'm so thankful to have that couple time back.

~Kristin Lambert, mother to Josh

My husband and I needed help as new parents usually do. The first night home from the hospital was a complete disaster. We even had to take turns sleeping since our newborn decided he would have none of that!! So, we did some research and ended up ordering this book. We absolutely loved it! After utilizing the tips, our son ended up sleeping a few solid hours a night. We were not sleep deprived either as new parents usually are. We could not believe it.

My husband and myself highly recommend "The Baby Sleep Coach" to new parents and parents of toddlers as well.

~Christie Wielenga, Mother to Shane

I thought my 18 month old son was going through the "terrible twos" early until I found The Baby Sleep Coach. After using her program, I realized that his lack of sleep was the real problem for his temper tantrums and bad behavior, not the terrible twos! He is now sleeping twelve hours straight at night and taking two hour naps during the day. And best of all I have my sweet baby back again. I could have never thought that sleep was so closely tied to his behavior. Thank you, thank you, thank you.

~Paula Sabatini, Mother to Jake

At the age of 11 weeks old, I am delighted to say that my triplets are sleeping twelve hours straight at night. They fall asleep on their own and are so happy when they awaken in the morning. I am so glad that I found The Baby Sleep Coach as early as I did. She provided me with simple tips and tricks that worked like magic to help my triplets develop good sleep habits from day one. I am grateful that I will not have to face sleep problems in the future. Thank you Baby Sleep Coach from a well rested mommy!

~Nicole Walsh, Mother to triplets, Rylee, Kelsey, & Cayden

Thank you ... From the first day I tried your program... it seems to be taking me in the right direction. My friend is pregnant with her first baby in February and I told her how fantastic your book was. Hopefully she will take me seriously and order your book too.

Like I said before, I just wish I would have come across this sooner. I would have been a lot happier. Sleep is so important for babies and their parents. You should really give seminars on this because I believe that with a little education parents would be aware of their feelings. Now I feel like I have a little more time to myself while he naps and I feel more like me.

~Nancy Friedman

Thank you so much! I am happy to say that last night my daughter had her best night ever! She woke up at 4:30 am but actually went back to sleep until 7 (I did have to feed her but she is still only 14 pounds). I am hoping we have turned a corner. I am thrilled with the progress we have made and thank you so much! I am a happier and better parent because of your help. We certainly will be passing your contact information along to all our friends and family having these types of problems.

~Kim Bell, Mother to Baby Girl

Our daughter, who is ten months this week had stopped sleeping through the night at about eight months. My wife and I tried everything, music, cradling, swaddling, rocking, etc. She would wake at 11:30 p.m., 1:45 a.m., and 5 a.m. like clockwork every night. It usually would take about thirty to ninety minutes to get her back to sleep. We would bring her in bed and she was happy, but very restless. After implementing The Baby Sleep Coach System, she went to bed by herself and slept through the night on the first night! I just want to say thank you for helping us get back to a normal routine!"

~Dr. Anthony Longo, Father to Gianna

Natalie is 4 months old. She sleeps very well since implementing your plan. She now falls asleep on her own at bedtime, and sleeps 11 to 12 hours straight every night!

~Leslie Simpson. Mother to Natalie (age 4 months)

Just wanted to send you a quick update. Things are really going very well. He is sleeping so much better. I can definitely tell a difference in his moods. Thanks for your help. He is now sleeping through the night and later in the morning!

~Amy Scott, Mother to Vincent (age 9 months)

The Baby Sleep Coach Book

How to Easily Get Your Baby to
Sleep Through the Night and Nap During
the Day in Seven Simple Steps

Dr. Heather Pizzo
Infant/Toddler Sleep Coach
www.babysleepcoach.com

Legal Disclaimer:

This program contains information and advice for parents. It was created as an aid to help parents establish healthy sleep patterns for their infants and/ or toddlers. Please note that this information is NOT intended to replace medical advice from your pediatrician and/or any other trained health care professional. It is recommended that you consult with your child's pediatrician before making any changes to your child's routine, or for any other matters that require medical attention or diagnosis.

Dedication

To my four boys, Logan, Ryan, Tristan, and Haydan. If it weren't for you, this book would have never come into existence. You were my inspiration, my trial and errors, and overall my successes. Lastly, to my loving husband, Chris, who suffered through my insanity and quest to again find sleep and a "normal" life with our four children.

Free Gift

As a special bonus for readers of this book, I'm offering an accompanying Baby Sleep Coach Quick Start and White Noise Audio (in mp3 format) for free.

To download this accompanying audio at no-cost, simply visit:

www.babysleepcoach.com/bonus.html

Dear Exhausted Parent,

If you're feeling frazzled, frustrated, and maybe even guilty because your baby won't fall asleep on his/her own and sleep through the night, pay very close attention to this.

Because what I have for you could be a very important turning point in how you feel about yourself as a parent, the bond you have with your child, and even your energy levels. I'll show you how starting tonight, you can restore peace to your home and finally enjoy your little one the way you'd love to do...just by "coaching" your baby to reliably fall asleep on their own and sleep through the night.

The good news is, unlike every other baby sleep program on the market, this is now being called...

"The Ultimate Breakthrough For Solving ANY Baby's Sleep Problems"

Why? Because **this is the ONLY method available that is completely customizable to YOUR baby's unique personality and YOUR natural parenting style**.

After all, babies weren't sent down from some "baby factory" as little identical clones, and one size does NOT fit all when it comes to your baby's sleep style!

I'm excited to share this with you, because it is remarkably easy to resolve your baby's sleep problems once and for all when you have the right methods at your fingertips. And when you do…

You AND Your Baby Will Be Happier, Healthier, and Even MORE In Love Than Before!

My name is Heather Pizzo. I've been dubbed the Baby Sleep Coach because I've successfully coached hundreds of desperate parents on exactly how to transform sleepless nights (for them AND their babies!) into peaceful slumbers in 6 days or less.

In this book, I'm going to show you how starting tonight, you can be on your way to connecting with your baby in a way that is not hindered by feelings of hopelessness, despair, and guilt for not being a good parent!

I know this is true, because it's already worked for me with my own four children and for many others too.

The Baby Sleep Coach System is a "first of it's kind" comprehensive program with a unique capability that makes it work like clockwork for ANY sleep problem.

My proprietary method stems from my belief that no two babies are alike, and therefore, no one system can work effectively for all children. This has been confirmed countless times by both personal experience, and my work with scores of parents.

After years of study and personal experience, **I've developed a flexible approach using what I call a "method selector tool" to instantly pinpoint what type of method would be most effective for you and your baby.**

Just by answering a series of simple questions, you can quickly zero in on the exact approach that will work for your particular situation. _There are no WRONG answers, because this is about your baby and you!_

You'll find there is a method that is perfect for your parenting style, your way of relating to your baby, and your baby's temperament. That means your whole family will be comfortable with the transition. And by following seven simple steps I'll guide you through…

It's easy, it's powerful, and it's effective. And you can start "training" your sweet baby to sleep starting tonight. It all starts with one simple decision to take action.

The only real question left is…

Do you sincerely want to see your baby sleeping peacefully through the night, EVERY night? If the answer is YES…

Then Read on to See What To Do Next…

This is one of those defining moments where you will always remember making such a smart decision as a parent, and truly providing the very best for your child.

It is my honor to share this life-changing journey with you.

To your baby's sweetest dreams,

Heather L Pizzo

Heather L. Pizzo, Psy.D.
Infant/Child Sleep Coach
www.babysleepcoach.com

Contents

1

Meet the Baby Sleep Coach

I have to warn you, after you have a baby your life will never be the same as before, but it does not have to be miserable. From the start, you as a parent play a vital role in the development of your infant's sleep patterns. Sleep problems in the first year of life are the most frequent complaints of parents to their pediatrician.

During the first year of life, 20% to 30% of infants manifest disrupted sleep serious enough to cause parents to seek professional assistance. During the toddler period, the rates of disturbance increase. Approximately one child in three up to four years of age will continue to awaken during the night and require assistance by a parent to return to sleep.

However, all children can be taught to be good sleepers. A coach by definition is one who trains someone in some aspect of his or her life. Essentially, you are your child's coach. Just as in little league or football, you need to teach your child the skills needed to fall asleep on their own and stay asleep.

I'm Dr. Heather Pizzo, also known as the Baby Sleep Coach, and I have spent years researching, analyzing, and comparing sleep coaching methods. Since babies are not born with manuals and appear to be very complex beings, I have created a guide to help you easily maneuver your way through the maze we call parenthood and get your baby to sleep.

I, too, was once a parent in your shoes. When my first child was born, I could have never imagined how sleep deprived as a new mother I would have been until it actually happened. My first son only liked to sleep for short periods of time (forty minutes or less.) I was exhausted and could not even carry out my daily tasks. I often found myself in tears and doubting my ability as a mother. Life with a new baby was not how I envisioned.

After much time spent surfing the internet, talking with other mothers and reading a few books, my darling bundle of joy really became a bundle of joy. After much experimenting, I had found the perfect combination of techniques or so I thought...

Then my second son was born and he was my worst nightmare! He would not sleep during the day unless I was holding him. And if I was holding him, he would only sleep for brief periods of time (thirty minutes or less). He was up many times throughout the night and would often not want to go back to sleep. He hated the swing, hated the bouncy seat, and hated the car!

It was then that I desperately began searching for a solution and came upon some age old wisdom that allowed me to develop The Baby Sleep Coach System. Within days, my second son began to sleep through the night for eleven to twelve hours straight. I was amazed at how my two children were so different in how I had to coach them to sleep. It was then that I decided to pursue my passion as an infant and child sleep coach and help other tired parents overcome or avoid the misery that goes along with not getting enough sleep.

I am now an infant/child sleep specialist who has coached many tired parents on how to develop good sleep patterns in their children. I have a doctoral degree in psychology and years of experience working with children. Above all, I have succeeded in getting many children to go to bed happily, nap well during the day, and sleep through the night, every night.

Starting tonight, I want to help you get your baby to sleep without having to spend excess time researching methods, and without the wasted money on numerous sleep books and poorly trained sleep consultants.

2

Why do Children Develop
Sleep Problems?

Research shows that twenty to thirty percent of all infants and toddlers will have some difficulty sleeping. Infants often have sleep problems during the first year of life. These include irregular sleep patterns, trouble getting to sleep, and waking at night. Sleep problems tend to continue or reappear in the preschool years and have been linked to childhood behavior problems, hyperactivity in children, psychiatric symptoms in adolescence and maternal depression.

Many parents feel that their children will not go to sleep unless they feed or rock them to sleep. This is because the child has only learned how to fall asleep by being fed or rocked. Persistent night awakenings in infants and toddlers usually reflect the child's inability to self-soothe back to sleep without parental attention.

It is important, however, that as a parent you help your child develop good sleep habits at an early age. If a child is not given the opportunity to develop strategies to fall and stay asleep on their own, they may become dependent on outside stimuli to assist them.

Infants need to be taught how to fall asleep. Recent research has shown that babies and toddlers are more securely attached and happier after sleep coaching. Babies who fall asleep on their own are more likely to fall asleep faster and become better able to soothe themselves to sleep. The best way to develop healthy sleep habits is to have a consistent bedtime routine and to put your infant into their bed while they are drowsy but awake.

Research finds infants who have not established good sleep patterns by eight months of age are likely to have frequent night awakening still at age three. One study found that when parents of four month old infants were encouraged to start putting their babies to bed while they were still awake, by nine months of age, these babies were sleeping much better than parents who waited until their babies were asleep in their arms before laying them in their cribs.

If you start sleep coaching early, you will be off to a good start to preventing sleep problems. Developing the ability to self-soothe will enable your baby to snooze for longer stretches and put himself back to sleep when he awakens in the night.

Sleep problems in babies create a vicious cycle in which lack of sleep effects parental happiness, which in turn effects parental relationships, which creates discord in the household, which in turn effects infant temperament.

How Do I Know If My Child Has a Sleep Problem?

Some sleep problems are immediately obvious to parents whereas others are not so obvious. Your child has a sleep problem if you can answer yes to any or all of the following questions:

❑ Does your child have difficulty falling asleep or staying asleep at night?

❑ Does your child take short catnaps throughout the day?

❑ Does your child appear overtired, irritable, or wound up during the day?

❑ Does your child need to be held all the time?

❑ Does your child wake up in a bad mood?

❑ Does your child reach developmental milestones later than average?

❑ Does your child constantly rub his eyes, pull on his ears, and/or yawn?

- [ ] Does your child fall asleep in the car or carriage almost every time you go out?

- [ ] Does your child fight naps?

- [ ] Does your child get less than the recommended amount of sleep for his/her age?

If you have answered yes to three or more questions above, your child is suffering from a sleep problem. Because sleep problems can have very significant effects on your child's health and behavior, it is very important that you as a parent take the next step in remedying the problem before it becomes an even bigger issue (or a lifelong issue). Please read on to learn more about sleep coaching your baby.

3

What is Sleep Coaching & When Can We Start?

Sleep coaching is the process of parents or caregivers helping a baby learn to fall asleep on their own at bedtime and stay asleep throughout the night. All babies normally wake during the night, but sleep coaching enables them to put themselves back to sleep without requiring the assistance of a parent. Therefore also allowing you a full night's sleep. Babies are not born with the ability to put themselves to sleep or self-soothe. Up until about the age of four months, babies' neurological and biological systems are underdeveloped and they rely on you for their every need. Therefore, they may not always be able to soothe themselves to sleep.

Sleep coaching methods were first formally introduced in 1959. Williams was the first in the field of sleep coaching to apply the method of extinction or more commonly known as the "cry it out" approach. Graduated extinction also known as the "modified cry it out" approach was first devised by Rolider and Van Houten as a more parent-friendly alternative to the "cry it out" approach. Sleep coaching methods have since evolved based on these original researchers' ideas. To date, all of the baby sleep books and programs on the market are based on this past research.

By the age of about three months, most babies have started to develop more regular sleep/wake cycles and have discontinued most of their night feedings. Sleep coaching can begin between the ages of four to six months of age, when most babies are capable of sleeping through the night. It is a general rule of thumb that most babies are capable of being able to sleep through the night without a feeding by the time they are four months old **and** fourteen pounds. Some babies begin to sleep through the night when they reach thirteen pounds. Please remember to age adjust for premature babies (i.e. Count the age from the approximate due date not from when they were born.)

One of the major problems of most sleep coaching approaches is that not enough attention is given to the importance of sleep and establishing a healthy sleep routine. Prevention of sleep problems if possible is optimal. Just because you cannot start formally sleep coaching your baby before the age of four months does not mean that you cannot start laying the path for healthy sleep habits. If you start early you may be able to minimize the amount of sleep coaching later on. For example, beginning around the age of six weeks, you can strengthen your baby's own biological rhythms by establishing a regular bedtime routine. This area will be covered in more depth later on.

Top 10 Reasons Why You Should Sleep Coach Your Baby

1. Sleep is the body's way of recharging its batteries. During sleep, the body repairs itself.

2. A baby's brain especially needs sleep. Scientists think that sleep may be the time when the brain sorts and stores information, replaces chemicals, and solves problems.

3. If your baby does not get enough sleep, he may not grow as well either. Researchers believe too little sleep can affect growth and the immune system.

4. When your baby does not get enough rest, he will become tired, cranky, and clingy.

5. Sleep problems are also a cause of daytime behavior problems.

6. Meltdowns at the end of the day are often a sign of an overtired child desperate for sleep.

7. Over stimulated infants have a difficult time calming down to rest.

8. Infants and toddlers who are sleep deprived are more demanding of their parents' attention, irritable, and learn less from their environment.

9. Infants and toddlers who get the proper amount of sleep, are happier, play well independently, and are better able to focus their attention and learn from their environment.

10. A baby who goes to sleep unwillingly or wakes frequently during the night can be highly disruptive to your marriage, other relationships and the harmony of your family.

4

How to Use this Guide

This guide is designed to be a thorough guide for all expectant parents and exhausted parents of infants and toddlers. Because it is meant to cover different stages of development, it can be used in different ways. **It does not have to be read from cover to cover.**

This guide is divided into thirteen chapters.

Chapters two and three will discuss why children develop sleep problems and go over the concept of sleep coaching.

Chapter five will provide you with background information necessary for understanding your child's sleep. It goes into detail about the importance of sleep, sleep basics, sleep characteristics by age, why children develop sleep problems, feeding and its relation to sleep, as well as information about crying.

Chapter Six will discuss naps, windows of opportunity and how to improve your baby's naps.

Chapter seven will provide you with detailed information about why babies cry.

Chapters eight and nine will provide you with guidelines for setting up a nursery and sleep safety tips, getting through the first four months, and provide you with information on establishing a healthy sleep routine during that time.

Chapters ten and eleven explore different types of sleep coaching methods as well as how to wean your baby off of sleep aids. Included here is the sleep coaching method selector tool. It will provide you with an individualized sleep coaching method that is right for you and your baby. These chapters also contain the seven simple steps to implement and carry out the methods.

Chapter twelve explains how to apply the baby sleep coach method to twins and multiples, as well as tips for synchronizing their sleep and feeding schedules.

Lastly, there is a **Frequently Asked Questions** section that covers issues that may interfere with or disrupt the process of sleep training children.

There are three ways in which you can use this guide. **For expectant parents,** I highly recommend that while you have the time and are not yet sleep deprived it would be very beneficial to read the book cover to cover. It is important that you understand all aspects of sleep and the sleep coaching process. By understanding the underlying principles of sleep, you will better be able to establish healthy sleep habits from the start and be prepared to combat any sleep troubles should they occur.

For parents of infants under four months of age, you can go right to chapters eight and nine. This will help you get through the early sleep deprived days. When you have more time and a clear head, please read through the other sections, especially chapter five.

For parents of infants and toddlers (over the age of four months to three years of age) with sleep struggles, go immediately to chapter ten. This will get you started immediately and on your way to sleep filled nights in six days or less.

For parents of toddlers over the age of three years of age with sleep struggles, go immediately to chapter eleven. This will get you started immediately and on your way to sleep filled nights in six days or less.

For parents of multiples with sleep struggles, go immediately to chapter ten or eleven and then proceed to read chapter twelve for more useful tips.

Remember, doing something is always better than doing nothing at all. It is never too late! It is important to understand the concept and importance of sleep. Therefore, I recommend that you read the entire book once you are well rested.

Please note, throughout this guide I have interchanged the words "he" and "she". This is simply done to include both genders in the guide. However, all the information contained in this book applies to both genders. In addition, I have used the titles "mom" and "dad" interchangeably. These refer to whomever may be coaching the child during the sleep learning process.

Lastly, as you read through this book, you my find some information repeated more than once. That's because I have created a book that does not have to be read cover to cover, therefore I repeated a few key points to be sure that all are able to find them.

5

Sleep Basics

Importance of Sleep

Sleep is very valuable for both you and your baby. Sleep is essential for your health, physical development, emotional well-being, and cognitive growth. Sleep helps our body and brain develop and grow. Sleep is similar to food. Our body needs sleep to grow and function just as it needs food to grow and survive. Both the quantity of your sleep as well as the quality of your sleep is equally as important.

Sleep influences every part of our life. Not only do parents have an impact upon the development of healthy sleep in children, but the children's sleep problems also affect the whole family. Sleep is influenced by both genetics and the environment. Sleep behavior is learned, and you are your baby's best teacher when it comes to establishing good sleep skills.

Just like you and me, infants need sleep in order to grow, develop and stay healthy. While a baby is asleep, the cells in his brain and body are multiplying rapidly and growth hormone is being produced. The body produces white blood cells in order for his immune system to properly fight off colds and viruses. Brain cell connections are rapidly expanding as well.

Sleep Background

Our sleep is regulated by an internal body clock, which is called a circadian rhythm. A baby's biological clock begins maturing around four to nine weeks of age. Internal biological clocks that regulate sleep-wake cycles are coordinated with recurring internal signals such as hunger, and with environmental cues, such as the light-dark cycle, and temperature. By six months of age, an infant's sleep closely resembles that of an adult.

Most of us alternate between REM sleep and non-REM sleep. REM, which stands for Rapid Eye Movement, is the period of sleep when we dream. During periods of REM sleep, infants may startle and twitch and their eyes will move beneath their eyelids. In the newborn, 50% of total sleep time is occupied by REM sleep, progressively shrinking to 25% in the adult.

Infants enter sleep through an initial active REM stage, in contrast to adults, who don't normally enter REM sleep until 90 minutes into the sleep cycle. Non-REM sleep is a deeper sleep, which has restorative functions. It is where the growing takes place. Non-REM sleep consists of four phases:

drowsiness, light sleep, deep sleep, and very deep sleep.

Babies make many sleeping sounds, from gurgles to grunts to cries. These noises do not always signal awakening. Being able to differentiate between these sleeping sounds and awake sounds is very important. There are times when your baby may go through a light phase of sleep and you may think that your baby is waking up. Do not immediately run to comfort her during this time. You will only awaken your baby and delay her from possibly going back to sleep.

A basic rest/activity cycle originates in fetal life. Newborns have irregular sleep cycles which take about six months to mature. The newborn sleeps an equal amount during the day and the night, and the sleep/wake cycles are organized around feedings. As the brain develops and becomes more mature, infants develop more regular, predictable sleep periods. As your infant's brain continues to mature, periods of sleep gradually become longer and more predictable.

Longer periods of sleep first develop during the night, and later extend to daytime naps. By the second month, longer stretches of night-time sleep occur and by six months the baby will have about twelve hours of sleep at night in addition to a couple of daytime naps. By six months of age, it typically takes an infant ten to twenty minutes to fall asleep.

Just like adults, many infants awaken briefly several times during the night throughout their first year of life and beyond. It is natural for a baby to briefly awaken during the night. This is the brain's way of "checking" the surrounding environment to make sure that everything is still safe and as it was previously. This is not a problem as long as your baby has not relied on you or some other sleep aid to soothe her to sleep initially. Her sleep environment when she is sleeping must be the same as when she falls asleep. Otherwise, she will awaken and her brain will send her a signal that something is wrong. For example, you rock your baby to sleep then place her in her bed. She then briefly awakens and her brain tells her that something is not right because you are no longer there rocking her to sleep. She then cries out to remedy the situation.

Uninterrupted sleep is the most restful and healthy kind of sleep. This type of sleep is known as consolidated sleep. Consolidation refers to the infant's ability to sustain sleep in a continuous fashion for an age-appropriate period of time before fully awakening. The establishment of a consolidated night sleep pattern in babies reflects brain maturation and may be disrupted in children with developmental problems.

Regulation of sleep refers to the ability of infants to transition smoothly from wakefulness to sleep. Struggles at bedtime and frequent nighttime awakenings represent disruptions of regulation and consolidation. Infants vary in the amount of sleep they need and the amount of time it takes to fall asleep.

The sleep cycle is a continuous twenty-four hour cycle. Each day directly impacts the next day. Skipping naps and allowing an infant to stay up late will affect what happens the following day. A baby will sleep more fitfully and wake up earlier when they are sleep deprived. The better rested you are, the easier it is to fall asleep and stay asleep, at any age. You are harming your child when you allow unhealthy sleep patterns to develop or continue.

According to sleep research, the length and quality of naps affect nighttime sleep, and nighttime sleep affects naps as well. A nap too late in the day will negatively affect nighttime sleep. If you miss the window of opportunity (the best time for your child to fall asleep), her adrenal glands will secrete a stress related hormone called cortisol into her body. This in effect will overstimulate her and make her appear as if she got a "second wind." She will be more difficult to console, cranky, and require a lot more of your attention. It will then be harder for her to fall asleep and stay asleep, and she will be more likely to wake at night and/or early the next morning.

Sleep Characteristics by Age

The first year of life is a time of major changes. When your baby is born, for the first few days all she seems to do is sleep. A newborn is usually awake for the first few hours after birth and then will often sleep for up to twenty-four hours after. She will most likely wake only for short periods of time to eat.

Newborns sleep a lot, typically fourteen to eighteen hours a day during the first week and twelve to sixteen hours a day by the time they are a month old. During the early months of your infant's life, he will sleep when he is tired. An infant cannot be forced to sleep when they do not want to sleep and you can do little to wake them when they are sleeping.

In the beginning, your newborn does not know the difference between day and night. No matter what, your newborn will wake up during the night. Often, a newborn will usually sleep anywhere from thirty minutes to four hours at a time. Newborns typically have about seven sleeping and waking periods equally spaced throughout the day and night. Therefore, they will wake up two to three times a night for a feeding. In addition, newborns awaken easily because they spend large amounts of sleep time in active sleep, a light sleep state.

Six Weeks to Three Months

By six weeks of age, your baby will begin to have a clear night/day sleep pattern. From four to eight weeks of age, your baby will sleep an average of fifteen to seventeen hours total. By eight to twelve weeks, your baby will sleep an average of fifteen hours a day. At about six weeks of age, night sleep becomes more organized and your baby may sleep four to six hours at night. He will be sleeping more at night and be more awake during the day. At this age, bedtime should start to be established between eight and nine o'clock.

By six to eight weeks, infants can usually only stay awake for one to two hours at a time. Daytime sleep takes longer to be established so napping will continue to be inconsistent. Many naps will be short, about forty minutes but they should gradually lengthen. Lastly, by six weeks, babies begin to differentiate their cries. Therefore it should be easier to determine why your baby is crying.

By eight to twelve weeks, your baby's biological clock starts to develop. Infants this age can still usually only stay awake for one to two hours at at time. However, sleep may become more regular and you may even be able to establish a routine.

Three to Four Months

By the third month, your baby should be sleeping an average of ten hours a night. She should be taking three naps a day for a total of five hours. At this point, nap length is variable. This is because the part of the brain that establishes regular naps has not fully developed. It is also at this time that babies' brains go through a big growth spurt and your baby will become extremely alert and distractible.

At about twelve weeks, the morning nap should become well established with your baby sleeping for about an hour to an hour and a half. A short time later, around sixteen weeks of age, the afternoon nap will become more established as well.

Four to Six Months

At four months, your baby should be able to sleep for eight to ten hours a night without a feeding. By six months of age, your baby should be sleeping ten to twelve hours a night without a feeding. At this time, your baby should not require more than one night feeding unless otherwise advised by your pediatrician. Most infants are able to start sleep longer stretches at night (ten to twelve hours) when they are four months **or** fourteen pounds.

Six to Nine Months

From six to eight months, your baby should be sleeping an average of eleven hours at night, and three and a half hours during the day broken into two daytime naps. Bedtime should be established between six thirty p.m. and seven thirty p.m. By six months of age, all night feedings should be eliminated. You can now offer your baby a small transitional object.

By six months, the third nap disappears. Your baby should now be taking a morning and an afternoon nap. The morning nap should take place about two and a half after wake up time and should last from one and a half to two hours long. There then should be three hours of awake time between the morning and the afternoon nap. The afternoon nap should last from one and a half to two hours. If your baby has napped poorly (less than an hour), she may need an additional brief third nap. This is considered an "emergency nap" and can be induced by a carriage or car ride, if necessary. Make sure that this nap is not too close to bedtime. Your baby needs at least two and a half to three hours of awake time before bedtime.

If you are experiencing difficulty with getting your baby to go down by himself for naps or bedtime, your baby is now old enough for the sleep coaching methods described in chapter ten.

Nine to Twelve Months

By the ninth month of age, your baby should be sleeping for eleven hours at night and for about three hours during the day. Your baby should still be taking two naps a day, a morning and an afternoon nap. Around nine months of age, the morning and afternoon nap should each last for about one to two hours.

As your baby approaches his first birthday, the length of these naps will decrease. Wake up time should be between six and seven thirty, and three hours of awake time should pass before the morning nap. In addition, there should be a three and a half hour time span between the morning nap and the afternoon nap. Baby's bedtime should continue to be between six thirty and seven thirty. If your baby's second nap lasts later into the afternoon, bedtime can be moved to eight o'clock.

Twelve to Eighteen Months

From twelve to eighteen months, your baby should be sleeping an average of eleven and a quarter hours a night with two naps during the day. The morning nap should be scheduled three to four hours after wake up time and the afternoon nap should be scheduled three to four hours after the morning nap. Each nap should be an average of one and a half hours long.

By eighteen months, most toddlers transition to one mid afternoon nap lasting two to two and a half hours long, approximately five to six hours after wake up time. Bedtime should be around seven o'clock but no later than eight o'clock depending on the wake up time from the afternoon nap. You do not want your baby to be awake longer than five to six hours between the afternoon nap and bedtime.

One and a Half to Two Years Old

By two years of age, your toddler should be sleeping an average of eleven hours at night, and taking one nap a day for about two hours. Your toddler will most likely wake up between six thirty and seven thirty in the morning. The nap should be scheduled six to seven hours after wake up time. Bedtime should be around seven and no later than eight o'clock. Once again, bedtime should be based on the afternoon nap. You do not want more than six to seven hours of awake time to elapse between the afternoon nap and bedtime.

Two to Five Years Old

Between the ages of two and three, your toddler should be sleeping an average of eleven hours at night, with a one and a half hour nap in the afternoon. You should also transition your child to a bed between the ages of two and a half to three. (I recommend waiting until your child is three years old.)

In addition, the afternoon nap disappears somewhere between three and four years of age. As the afternoon nap is phased out, children may nap some days and not others. This is okay, as long as the nap does not interfere with bedtime. A child of this age, if she is continuing to take a nap, should not be sleeping past two-thirty p.m. in order to preserve her bedtime. By age four, your toddler should be sleeping an average of eleven and a half hours at night.

By age five, your child should be sleeping an average of eleven hours at night. Bedtimes throughout these years should still continue to be between seven and eight o'clock with a wake up time between six and seven o'clock. After the age of four, children usually no longer require a nap. However, it is important that you still set aside a time of the day, usually after lunch where your child has some quiet time. Quiet time could consist of reading books, or watching a video, as long as your child is resting during this activity. Quiet time should last for at least forty-five minutes to an hour. This will also provide you with some quiet time for yourself.

Feeding and Its Relation to Sleep

Newborns grow rapidly, and their stomachs digest quickly. Newborns need to be fed every two and a half to four hours, sometimes more. Many pediatricians recommend that parents should not let a newborn sleep longer than three or four hours without a feeding. Breast fed babies often nurse eight to twelve times a day. Bottle fed babies often eat six to eight times a day. Wake your baby if he or she goes more than four hours without a feeding during the day. Babies who go too long without food during the day often wake up and feed more at night. In addition, there are times in your infant's development where he will go through growth spurts and exhibit signs of hunger more often.

Make sure that your baby is taking in the proper amount at each feeding. If you are breastfeeding your baby, let her take your first breast until it is drained (she pulls away), then offer her the second breast if she wants more. During the first ten to fifteen minutes, your baby will get the foremilk, which is higher in lactose. Next comes the hindmilk, which is fattier and more filling.

Babies who feed more often than every two hours often nurse for just a few minutes at a time and miss out on the hindmilk. This can make a baby more gassy and fussy because she is getting a disproportionate amount of lactose. At the next feeding, offer your baby the opposite breast if she did not feed from it or offer your baby the breast with which you last fed if she fed from both previously. In addition, as a nursing mother, monitor your diet. Try to eliminate any forms of caffeine such as coffee, tea, soda, and chocolate. Caffeine can have an effect on your baby's sleep through your breast milk.

If you are bottle-feeding your baby, make sure that your baby feeds every three to four hours during the day with no less than three hours in between feedings. Generally, babies who have not started solids need approximately two to two and a half ounces of formula per pound of body weight every twenty-four hours. Take this number and divide it by the number of feedings during the day to get the amount of ounces you need to put in each bottle. (i.e. A baby is fifteen pounds so multiply fifteen by two which equals thirty, or fifteen times two and a half equals thirty-seven and a half. So the baby should be taking in thirty to thirty-seven and a half ounces across six to eight feedings during the day.) It is a good idea to always put a half an ounce more in each bottle so that you ensure that your baby is getting enough.

The best way to determine if your baby is hungry is to look for signs. A baby will 'root' (turn her head and open her mouth), bring her hands to her mouth and/or make sucking motions. You will be able to sense if your baby needs more because he will finish quickly and then look around for more. Your baby may not take the same amount at each meal. Do not force your baby to finish a bottle, feed him as long as he is eager to drink.

Be careful not to overfeed your baby. Crying may be caused by belly cramps from overeating or swallowing too much air during feeding. Babies give cues during feeding that indicate how hungry they are. Pay attention to these cues to help determine when your baby has had enough to eat.

A baby who is hungry will take the bottle or easily latch onto the breast and suck continuously. A baby who is getting full during a feeding will take longer pauses between sucking. A baby who has had enough to eat will turn away from the breast or bottle and not want to suck.

The composition of infant formula is very different from breast milk so it will take your baby almost twice as long to digest formula. A breastfed baby needs at least two and a half to three hours to digest a full feeding and a bottle fed baby needs three to four hours to digest a full feeding. If you feed your baby before she really needs it, she will most likely only take an ounce or two and will need a feeding again in a couple of hours. This is more likely to lead to gas and discomfort for your baby, as well as interfere with sleep. If your baby wants to suck in between feedings, offer her a pacifier. You can use a pacifier to stall feedings as necessary.

Because it will take more time for your baby to digest formula, he may also sleep for longer periods of time. In addition, babies digest formula more slowly than breast milk, so a baby who is getting formula may need fewer feedings than one who breastfeeds. However, breast milk and formula contain the same number of calories per ounce. Therefore, it is a myth that breastfed babies will take longer than bottle fed babies to sleep through the night.

During the first month, your infant should have six to eight wet diapers a day and have at least two bowel movements daily. This will assure you that your infant is getting enough to eat. By two months of age, most babies have established regular feeding schedules. Bottle-fed babies tend to eat about every three to four hours, and breast-fed babies nurse approximately every three hours.

Once you start solids, your baby's daily intake of formula should gradually decrease to about twenty four ounces per day. Solid foods should not be introduced too soon (at around four to six months). The closer to six months the better, although some bigger babies require the introduction of solid foods closer to four months of age. It is a common myth that feeding your baby cereal before bed will get him to sleep longer at night. Giving your baby cereal too early may actually cause him to cry from stomach discomfort and may lead to allergies in the future. (As always, please consult with your pediatrician first.)

It is best to try to feed your baby upon waking if possible. This will decrease the chance that your baby will fall asleep while feeding. In addition, it will help break the association between feeding and sleeping. When you baby is really young (under three months), it's all right if she falls asleep while eating sometimes. It's going to happen. Just try to not let it become a habit. As your baby gets older, she will naturally have more awake time after a feeding.

To keep your child awake while eating you can:

- Rub his head
- Sing to him
- Make eye contact with him
- Change your baby's position while feeding
- Change the diaper in the middle of a feeding
- Talk to your baby
- Tap the end of the bottle lightly (if bottle fed)

If a bottle fed baby feeds too slowly, it may because the nipple is screwed on too tightly or because the nipple size is too slow. Both situations can make feeding very tiring for a baby and he may fail to complete his feed or fall asleep midway through a feeding, resulting in a consistently hungry and fussy baby. The following guide will help you determine if your baby is taking the appropriate time to finish his bottle.

- ❑ twenty to forty minutes for newborn to three months
- ❑ fifteen to thirty minutes for babies three to six months

❑ ten to twenty minutes for babies over six
months

It is very important not to misinterpret all
crying and fussing for hunger. All cries do not signal
hunger. Babies cry for other reasons and should not
be fed every time they cry or fuss. Make sure you go
down the list of possibilities: Is your baby cold/hot?,
Is your baby tired or overstimulated?, Is your baby
sick?, Does your baby's diaper need to be changed?,
or Is your baby bored or under stimulated? It is very
important that you decipher your baby's cries and
make sure that they are that of hunger, not something
else.

If you continue to feed your baby every time
he cries, he will develop a "snacking" habit. He will
want to nurse/feed continuously around the clock.
This is not good for you or your baby. It will not allow
your baby to get the proper sleep he needs and it will
be very exhausting for you. Try changing his diaper,
moving his position or making sure that he is not
tired. Learning to recognize your baby's cries will also
be very helpful. The following chart will help you
decipher your baby's cries.

If your baby's cry sounds like...	Then he is more than likely...
A rhythmic, cry-pause-cry-pause pattern that is often preceded by finger sucking, lip smacking, or turning of the head (less shrill and seems more demanding than desperate)	Hungry
A whiny cry with a possible whimper or moan and ends abruptly as soon as your baby is picked up	Bored
A wail that builds up in intensity and has a nasal quality	Tired
A prolonged cry that sounds, whiny, nasal and low pitched	Sick
A sudden shrill or a high-pitched shriek and is inconsolable despite your efforts to soothe	In pain

Don't worry if you are having a hard time deciphering between your baby's cries in the beginning. It may take up to three months for you to really get to know your baby and his cries and that is okay.

Lastly, I suggest keeping a daily feeding log. Mark down each time your baby eats as well as minutes nursed or ounces fed. Please see Appendix B for an example chart and Appendix A for blank charts.

6

Naps

Besides working on nighttime sleep, it is very important to work on daytime sleep. Naps develop between twelve and sixteen weeks of age. A morning nap occurs first followed several weeks later by the afternoon nap. At the age of four months, your baby will begin to settle into a sleep schedule and her napping will become more regular. Naps are very important and will continue to keep your child well rested. Timing of the naps is always based on the baby's wake time. Naps problems are harder to solve than nighttime problems.

The major way to prevent sleep problems from developing is to focus your efforts on helping your baby nap during the day. Babies have times during the day when they get sleepy and it is the optimum time to put them to sleep. These periods are often referred to as "windows of opportunity" and it is the easiest time for your baby to fall asleep and stay asleep. Do not let your baby become overtired. It will make it more difficult for your baby to get to sleep, make her more fussy, and disrupt her natural sleep cycle. As your baby grows, these "windows of opportunity" will become more predictable and longer.

Create a nap routine that is simple but similar to your bedtime routine so that your child will be cued that it is time to sleep. Start the routine twenty minutes before the desired nap time. By about four months of age, you want your baby napping in the crib for most of his naps. Napping requirements and schedules significantly change over the first year as your baby grows and develops. Refer to the chart on the following page when planning your baby's nap times.

An Overview of Recommended Windows of Wakefulness for Naps by Age

Age	To First Nap	To Second Nap	To Third Nap
0-3 mos.:	No more than 1 to 2 hours of wakefulness		
3-4 mos.:	1 to 2 hours	2 hours	2 hours
4-6 mos.:	2 hours	2 ½ hours	2 ½ hours
6-9 mos.:	2 ½ hours	3 hours	N/A
9 -12 mos.:	3 hours	3 ½ hours	N/A
12-18 mos.:	3 ½ hours	3 ½ to 4 hours	N/A
18–24 mos.:	4-5 hours	N/A	N/A
2 yrs.:	6 hours	N/A	N/A
3 – 5 yrs.:	7 hours	N/A	N/A

7

The Truth Behind the Tears

Perfect timing when putting a baby down to sleep produces no crying. Crying is the consequence of becoming overtired and / or overstimulated. Your baby has no way to communicate other than crying. It is important to remember crying can signify hunger, pain, discomfort, frustration, or even boredom. Responding to a baby's every cry with nursing or a bottle is not teaching your baby about communication.

Crying is not always bad. It is a way for your baby to express themselves, and let off steam. According to the American Academy of Pediatricians, "all babies cry, often without any apparent cause. Newborns routinely cry a total of one to four hours a day. It is not unnatural to let your baby cry for a little bit. No mother can console her child every time he cries; so don't expect to be a miracle worker with your baby."

If you however miss that window of opportunity, your baby will most likely cry when being coached to sleep. Babies will often go through a cycle of three distinct cries.The first cry is the Peak Cry. This cry is a very intense and hysterical cry. It is by far the hardest to listen to. However, this cry is often the shortest lasting only about 20 minutes or less.

The second cry is the Chanted Cry. This cry comes after the Peak Cry. It is an on again off again cry that sounds almost rhythmic and constant. Initially the Chanted Cry starts out very loud but then gradually becomes softer. This type of cry is the longest. It may last for 30 minutes or more during the initial days of sleep coaching. However, this cry is your baby's signal to you that he is trying to put himself to sleep. Try not to intervene during this time.

Lastly, there is the Almost Asleep Cry. This comes after the Chanted Cry and before your baby falls asleep. It usually sounds like one soft whimper type of cry or may even be one loud shriek before falling asleep.

Sleep coaching does not mean ignoring your baby's communication. Sometimes babies need to cry in order to wind down to fall asleep. A recent study by the by the American Academy of Sleep Medicine (2006) found that a few tear-filled nights (a.k.a. "crying it out") during sleep coaching will not harm your baby or produce any negative long-term effects. In fact, the studies revealed that infants who went through sleep coaching were more secure and predictable, and cried and fussed less, than those who weren't coached. You give your baby plenty of love and attention everyday. He or she will know that you still love them even if you do not respond to their every cry.

It is important to realize that you are not hurting your baby by letting him or her cry for specified periods of time. The first few times may be difficult but he will quickly learn to fall asleep on his own. In the long run, your baby will cry less, and both you and your baby will be happier overall. In many cases, by letting their baby cry, parents end a cycle of ongoing suffering for both them and the baby. Parents also report an overall general improvement in the baby's behavior and mood. Falling asleep is a learned behavior that must be taught. It is very important to be consistent in your method. The more consistent you are the faster your baby will learn.

8

Setting the Sleep Stage

Setting up the Nursery

Congratulations on the impending birth or birth of your new baby. This is a great time in a parent's life and because you have taken the initiative to establish a healthy sleep routine from the start you will also be better able to enjoy this time.

The Bed

Initially it is important to decide where your baby is going to be sleeping, whether it is in your bedroom or in his or her own bedroom. I would highly recommend putting your baby in her crib or bassinet in her own room once she reaches three months. The reason why I would recommend this is because babies are not sound sleepers. The noises, gurgles, and grunts of your baby may keep you from getting quality sleep, and in addition, you may inadvertently keep your baby from getting quality sleep. In addition, your baby establishes earlier that his crib and his room are for sleeping. However, it is okay if you choose to keep your baby in your room for the first few months, as this is usually more convenient for you in the beginning.

In today's age, with the use of baby monitors, it is very easy to hear your baby from their room, when necessary. I highly recommend purchasing a video monitor. Although these monitors are higher priced than your normal sound only baby monitor, they are worth their weight in gold. By being able to see your baby, you can be assured that he is okay when he's sleeping or stirring without running into his room to further disturb him. In addition, you will be able to tell when he falls asleep and wakes up. (It is not always easy to tell because some babies will hang out in their beds quietly.)

The one sleep arrangement that I would not recommend is co-sleeping or bed sharing. A review of the literature has suggested that co-sleeping is hazardous for the baby. One risk associated with co-sleeping is suffocation.

In addition, co-sleeping may lead to lighter infant sleep and increased night-awakenings. The U.S. Consumer Product Safety Commission (CPSC) and the American Academy of Pediatrics (AAP) warns parents not to place their infants to sleep in adult beds, stating that the practice puts babies at risk of suffocation and strangulation. Instead the AAP recommends that parents have their newborns sleep in the same room as them but on a separate sleep surface, such as a bassinet, playpen or crib. This makes it convenient for you to feed the baby in the middle of the night as well as keep an eye on him.

Your baby's crib should be free of any stimulating toys or mobiles, and the nursery should be painted in soothing pastel colors. (One article that I came across stated that a baby's room that is painted yellow may actually make them cry more.) A baby needs to know that his bedroom is for sleeping and may become over stimulated if his crib is filled with toys and bright colors. Plan to place your baby down to sleep in the same place for naps and bedtime.

Sleep Environment

In addition, invest in room darkening shades to help block out any unnecessary light that may impede sleep. (Darkness triggers the brain to release melatonin, a sleep hormone.) It is not necessary to install a night light. Your baby is pretty accustomed to a dark environment (the womb). If your baby seems calmer with a night light or you enjoy having it in the room then it is okay to use. However, make sure that it is a dim night light. Some sensitive babies or babies with colic may do better without the night light for the first few months. A white noise machine or fan is also necessary as a way to block out any environmental noise that may impede sleep.

Keep your baby's room temperature around sixty eight to seventy two degrees, unless you have a preterm infant or newborn weighing less than eight pounds; then you might want to increase the temperature by a few degrees. A sharp drop in body temperature induces sleep, which is often why a bath is recommended before bed.

Make sure you dress your baby appropriately for bed. As a general guide, dress and cover your infant in as much, or as little, clothing as you would put on yourself. Remember to accommodate for the blankets that you would use as well. Babies do not usually have the ability to keep blankets on until over the age of twenty four months. In addition, using blankets under the age of twelve months is a S.I.D.S. risk. Babies who are overheated tend to be more restless as well. Usually a light sleeper and a onesie for warmer weather (in air condition) and a fleece sleeper and onesie for colder weather. You can feel your baby's feet and neck to see if he's cold.

Sleep Safety Tips

- Always place your baby to sleep on his or her back, even during nap time.
- Do not smoke around your baby.
- Place baby on a firm mattress in an approved crib. Avoid using an old or used crib or cradle. For the most recent safety recommendations, visit the U. S. Consumer Product Safety Commission at www.cpsc.gov.
- Make sure the mattress fits tightly in the crib or cradle without any gaps to the side
- Remove soft, fluffy bedding and stuffed toys from your baby's sleep area.
- Use a sleep sack instead of a blanket.

- Don't overdress your baby by putting too many layers of clothing or blankets on your baby.
- Keep the bedroom at a comfortable sleeping temperature, usually between 68 and 72 degrees Fahrenheit.
- Do not put your baby to sleep near a window, window blinds, cords, or curtains.
- Never tie a pacifier to your baby with a string, ribbon, or cord.
- May sure all caregivers know and follow the above tips

A word about infant sleep positioning and Sudden Infant Death Syndrome (S.I.D.S.). The American Academy of Pediatricians recommends that parents and caregivers place healthy infants on their backs when putting them down to sleep. Recent studies have shown an increased incidence of S.I.D.S. in infants who sleep on their stomachs.

 **9**

Establishing Healthy Sleep Habits
The First Four Months

The Adjustment Period (a.k.a Womb Withdrawal)

If you are reading this book before your baby is born or if your baby is under four months of age, this is the best time to establish healthy sleep habits. By starting early, you are more likely to avoid any problems in the future and minimize the amount of time your baby spends crying. Overall, you will have an overall happier healthier baby and you will be happier as well.

The first three months after a baby is born is often referred to as the fourth trimester (referring to a continuation of the three trimesters of pregnancy.) Babies when they are born have to adapt to life outside of the womb.

This is a huge change for them as they were accustomed to having everything provided for them. They lived in a consistently warm dark environment, were lulled to sleep by their mother's constant movement, and were continuously nourished. Now upon entering the world, they must learn to regulate their body temperature, obtain food, and learn to soothe themselves to sleep. Not only is it a huge adaptation for your baby but you as parents also.

When babies are born, they do not have the neurological ability to soothe themselves to sleep when they are tired. Babies are born before their brain is fully developed. If babies stayed in the womb until their brains were more mature, they would not be able to fit through the birth canal. Therefore, this ability does not occur to around the fourth month of life.

Calming the Fussy Baby

Keeping your baby awake for too long or exposing her to too much noise or activity could lead to over stimulation. She will then have a harder time falling asleep, staying asleep, and become fussy. However, if your baby does become over stimulated the following advice will be of great help to you.

The best way to comfort or calm your baby during the first three months of life is to recreate the womb. Below are some tips that will help recreate the womb and soothe your baby when he is fussy.

Recreating the Womb

When recreating the womb experience you have to visualize how your baby felt in the womb.

There are six ways in which you can recreate the womb experience.

These methods should be used when a baby is fussy, over stimulated, or will not go to sleep on her own. Each of these can be used in conjunction with one another, or separately. Most of the time it is best to combine some or all of them, however sometimes too much may frustrate an already over stimulated baby.

Swaddling

The first method you can use to calm a baby less than four months of age is swaddling. Experts believe that it helps babies relax because it is reminiscent of the womb. In addition, swaddling helps keep babies from startling themselves awake with their involuntary reflexes.

To swaddle your baby, spread a receiving blanket out flat, with one corner folded over. Lay your baby face up on the blanket, with his head resting on the folded corner. Wrap one corner over his body and tuck it beneath him. Bring the bottom corner up over his feet tucking it in behind his other shoulder and back, and then wrap the opposite corner around him tucking it into the front, leaving only his head and neck exposed. Allow enough pressure for comfort but do not make it too tight as to cut off his circulation. There are also special blankets that you can use that are sold specifically for swaddling.

Many parents often comment how their babies "hate" swaddling. They often misinterpret their baby's squirming during swaddling for dislike. This is not the case and I highly encourage swaddling as it allows your baby to sleep better and for longer periods of time. Young babies do not have great control over their arms and are therefore awakened by the flailing of their arms, especially now with the "back to sleep" recommendation.

Sound Machine

In the womb, the sounds your baby hears are equivalent to the sound level of a vacuum cleaner. Therefore, babies are accustomed to a constant level of sound and may become upset when they are left in a quiet room to sleep. Place a sound machine or fan in your baby's room when they are going to sleep, sleeping, and/or over stimulated. The steady background hum will calm your baby and will also screen out any outside sounds. Make sure that the volume of the noise machine is equivalent to that of a vacuum. However, keep it at least six feet from where your baby is sleeping.

Sucking

Most babies are born with a strong desire to suck. Fetuses actually start sucking in the womb between fourteen and sixteen weeks of age. During the first few months, you can offer your baby a pacifier whenever needed. After three to four months or age, however, try to wean your baby off of it as soon as possible. You do not want it to become a sleep aid.

Motion

The movement of a swing, car, stroller, vibrating bouncy seat, or sling can help babies fall asleep and stay asleep longer. Swinging motions or other movement mimic the movement your baby felt inside the womb. Swinging works best when your baby is already in a somewhat calm state.

Try swaddling your baby first and rocking your baby in your arms before placing him in the swing. Do not put a screaming baby in the swing. It will not work. You will just end up with a screaming, swinging baby. In addition, make sure the seat is reclined as far as it goes and use the fastest speed. (Please remember as with any advice, consult with your doctor before using a swing.) Most infants, however, can be placed in the swing after three weeks of age.

Lighting

An overtired or over stimulated baby can be calmed with dimmed lighting. Remember they spent nine months in the dark! It is always important to dim the lighting during the evening hours as well. This will signal to the baby that bedtime is coming and aid in the adjustment of their natural circadian rhythms.

Position

Lastly, there is a recommended position, which almost always calms a fussy baby. Hold your baby sideways in your arms with her back facing your stomach and her stomach facing outward so that ultimately she is lying sideways. Lastly, support your baby's head with your hand. Babies are comforted by this position. In the womb, they were used to being curled up on their side. (Always remember, however, place your baby to sleep on his back.)

Sleep Coaching Under Four Months

The first important step you can take in establishing healthy sleep habits is to help your baby differentiate his days from his nights. A newborn baby sleeps approximately sixteen to eighteen hours per day and this sleep is distributed evenly over six to seven brief sleep periods. By helping your baby distinguish his days from his nights will enable him to lengthen his sleep periods during the nights. Long stretches of sleep develop first, followed by longer naps during the day.

Begin to teach the difference between night and day from the start by keeping nighttime feedings as subdued as possible. Do not turn on the lights and keep diaper changes short and change only when necessary. It is also recommended to use warm wipes or a warm washcloth. Do NOT play with your baby at this time and keep your nighttime interactions short and uninteresting.

In the evening, dim the lights in the room(s) in which your baby will be in as a cue to signal their bodies that night is approaching. In the beginning, have your baby take his daytime naps in a lit room and darken the room for night sleep. During the day, keep your baby in well-lit rooms during his awake times. Try and schedule your daily outings during your baby's "alert" times. Remember babies this age can only stay awake for forty-five minutes to one hour before needing to go back to sleep. (This includes time spent feeding.)

Do not respond to your baby's every cry by feeding him or her. Make sure that it is really hunger. Consider the time and/or amount of the last feeding, time spent awake, and check his or her diaper. Babies cry for reasons other than hunger. It is a general rule of thumb that breast fed babies are not fed less than every two hours between feedings and bottle fed babies are not fed less than three hours after the start of the previous feeding. Do not let your baby go more than four hours without a feeding during the day.

Make sure that your baby is eating enough at each feeding. A good formula for a bottle fed baby is two to two and a half ounces multiplied by body weight equals number of ounces in a twenty-four hour period. Then divide that number by the number of bottles in a day.

Breast fed babies should be nursing eight to twelve times a day with no more than twenty to thirty minutes total on both breasts. You can tell if your breast fed baby is getting enough milk if she has several periods of swallowing during each feeding, if your baby is having bowel movements regularly, and he is gaining weight. Between the fifth day and the end of your baby's third or fourth month, he should be gaining an ounce every day.

Starting early and being consistent are the keys to establishing good habits. You can set the proper sleep environment so that your baby can fall asleep on his own. If you take the proper steps for establishing healthy sleep habits and watch your baby for signs of sleepiness it is possible to put a baby down to sleep with little or no fussing.

Begin to watch your baby for signs of sleepiness. At this age, signs of sleepiness include decreased activity, quieting down, loss of interest in people, looking dazed, fussing, and/or yawning. Babies under four months of age cannot stay awake longer than one to two hours before they need to return to sleep. Some babies can only stay awake for forty-five minutes. It is important that you place your baby down at the proper time to ensure that he will transition to sleep easily. Always keep one eye on the clock and one eye on your baby.

Try not to over stimulate your baby. Babies this young can become over stimulated very easily. (Remember almost every sight, sound, and smell is new for them.) An over stimulated baby will cry intensely as a way to block out the world around him, as this is the only way he knows how to.

Babies less than six weeks old go to sleep very late at night. By six weeks of age begin to look for signs of drowsiness as your baby may begin going to bed a little earlier. At around one month of age start by establishing a bedtime routine. The half hour before bedtime is very important. At this age, it may only consist of a bath or sponge bath, changing into pajamas, and feeding. This routine helps signal to your baby that it is time for sleep.

It is important that your baby be put to sleep before he reaches the point of exhaustion. (When your baby is exhibiting signs of tiredness, do not make eye contact, it may make him more alert.) Put your baby to sleep when she is drowsy but awake. You want to always try to put your baby in her bed to sleep when she is tired. I know that it is sweet to hold a sleeping baby but try not to make a habit of it.

Avoid putting your baby to bed with a pacifier if possible. Pacifiers should only be used to satisfy your baby's need to suck and to comfort him. However, if your baby falls asleep with the pacifier, it is okay to use until the age of four months. Newborns often fall asleep while feeding, and that is okay. At this age, it is not necessary to wake your baby.

At around six to eight weeks, try stretching the length of naps by giving your baby about ten minutes to fall back asleep, even if they are fussing or crying. Your baby should be taking three to four naps a day. Continue putting your baby down to bed drowsy but awake and continue swaddling your baby for all sleep periods. During the day, you still want to wake him after four hours without a feeding and continue to follow the F.A.S.T. plan as described in the next section. By end of second month (around eight weeks) you should discontinue any sleep that involves motion (i.e. swing, car seat, stroller).

You want to begin to increase the time between his feeding intervals to four hours, if you aren't doing so already. You can do this by distracting your baby. Some ways to distract your baby include using a pacifier, playing with or entertaining your baby, or putting your baby in a bouncy seat or swing. (Just remember not to let your baby fall asleep unless he's due for a nap.) As you stretch the time between feedings you will find that your baby will consume more at each feeding.

When you know your baby is tired and needs to sleep, you can further begin to implement some sleep training strategies at the age of eight weeks old. For example, when trying to get your baby to sleep you can either sit/lay by his side and soothe him to sleep on his bed or you can also let him cry/fuss for up to five minutes as long as you know that he is not hungry, sick or has a dirty diaper.

Around eight weeks, you can also begin to work on lengthening the period that you baby sleeps at night. According to the American Academy of Pediatricians, by two months or twelve pounds most babies no longer need a middle of the night feeding because they are consuming more during the day and their sleeping patterns have become more regular.

This means that your baby can now most likely go without a feeding for seven to eight hours.

Many babies drop the middle of the night feeding on their own between their seventh and ninth week. Babies that hang onto their middle of the night feeding may need a little extra encouragement. Take note of any feedings between the hours of eleven at night and six in the morning and your baby's natural night feeding patterns. For each feeding, gradually reduce the number of ounces/minutes nursed starting with the first of the two feedings (if there are two). To do this, keep track of how many ounces (or minutes nursed) your baby is taking in at night. If you are not sure of the amount of ounces (or minutes nursed) it is better to overestimate [i.e. if your baby drinks six ounces (nurses fifteen minutes) one feeding and four ounces (ten minutes) the next, it is better to use the six ounces (fifteen minutes).]

When your baby awakens for a feeding, take him out of bed and feed him in a chair. Give him one half ounce less each night (or nurse one minute) less each feeding. Continue to decrease by one half ounces (one minute nursing) each night until he is weaned off of the middle of the night feeding(s) and is taking in all his calories between the hours of eleven p.m. and six a.m. If your baby continues to waken during this time and he has proved to you that he can go through the night without this feeding, use other the other methods described above to get him back to sleep.

Around three months of age, naps become more structured and babies become less portable for naps. Arrange your activities around her nap schedule and try to have your baby sleep in her crib for all naps. Babies this age need to return to sleep for their first nap within one to two hours of waking for the day. No more than two hours of awake time should pass between your baby's first and second nap and second and third nap. Your baby should be moved out of the bassinet and into his room by the end of the third month if you have not done so already.

At about twelve weeks, the morning nap should become well established with your baby sleeping for about an hour to an hour and a half. It is a good idea to begin a nap schedule starting with the morning nap because it is the first one to develop. As your baby begins to sleep for longer stretches at night, her morning nap will most likely become shorter (about an hour). A short time later, around sixteen weeks of age, the afternoon nap will become more established as well.

Your baby will take a short third afternoon nap (forty-five minutes to an hour). If you need to run errands during a nap, this is the nap to run errands during. The third nap is variable and often balances out the first two. Between your baby's last nap and his bedtime, he may now be able to stay awake for three hours if well rested.

A real bedtime should be established during this month. In addition, a structured bedtime routine should be performed nightly (i.e. bath, pajamas on, lullaby, bottle). Bedtime should be between eight and nine o'clock p.m. Most infants are able to start sleep longer stretches at night (ten to twelve hours) when they are four months **or** fourteen pounds. If your baby is not doing so yet, continue to follow the method as described in the previous section for transferring nighttime feedings to the day. In addition, feed your baby before bed and follow his lead after that. Do not wake him for a late evening feeding if he does not awaken on his own.

Between three and four months of age, you also want to discontinue swaddling your baby. To do this, I recommend swaddling your baby with one arm out for a few nights, followed by both arms out. If you feel that your baby is not yet ready to be unswaddled, try again in a few weeks. However, make sure that your baby is sleeping unswaddled by four and half months of age.

Continue to use your previous methods (as described above) for getting your baby to sleep. However, you want to avoid repeatedly picking up and putting down your baby as this will further agitate a baby at this age. It is okay to pick your baby up once to soothe him but after that try soothing him by the side of his crib without picking him up.

Remember to observe the windows of opportunity and get your baby to sleep when necessary. You want to avoid the overtired state. Continue to keep one eye on the clock and one eye on your baby for signs of sleepiness.

Up until now, you may have rocked your baby or given her a pacifier and she slept for hours without waking up. Between the ages of three to four months old, your baby is now sleeping more like an adult. Now when he falls asleep, instead of entering deep sleep, he enters a lighter sleep first. The beginning of the night is your baby's deepest sleep and after about the first five hours, he will cycle between light and deep sleep, but not as deep as the beginning of the night. This is where issues with night wakings come into play. If your baby needs your help to go to sleep in the beginning of the night, sometime after midnight or so, he will continue to need your help every one or two sleep cycles (that means every forty-five to ninety minutes).

That is why if you continue to help him fall asleep, he is more likely to wake up when you put him down because he has not reached his level of deeper sleep yet. It is at this time that you should put your baby down drowsy but awake every time you place him to sleep. By doing so, you are giving him the opportunity to develop self-soothing skills and to learn how to fall asleep unassisted. However, some babies learn quicker than others. If you feel that your baby is having difficulty, try putting him down drowsy but awake again at another time when he is a little older.

Babies this age may still awaken early (between five and six a.m.) for a brief feeding and return to sleep. Treat this as you would a night waking, not a nap. Feed your baby in a dimly lit room with very little stimulation and return him to bed. (Phase out this feeding by six months of age.)

Most children will awaken to start their day between six and eight a.m. You never want to start your baby's day before six a.m. because he will continue to wake up earlier and earlier to enjoy your company. Lastly, it is during this time that most babies are big enough for night time diapers. I highly recommend using these diapers at night to ensure that your baby stays dry and comfortable and is not awoken early by a leaky diaper.

The F.A.S.T Plan

It is best for both you and your baby to establish a "routine." By establishing a routine, your baby's circadian rhythms will develop, you will better be able to interpret your baby's cries, and you will have an overall easier first few months. I recommend following a Feeding, Activity, Sleep, Time for You plan, or as I call it the F.A.S.T. plan. (FAST because you'll be amazed at how fast time goes when following this plan.)

<u>Feeding</u>

You want to avoid feeding your baby right before a nap. By doing so you will create a suck/feed to sleep connection. When your baby awakens for a nap or for the day you want to offer your baby a bottle or nurse your baby. It is at this time that they will be most alert and therefore will feed best. Your baby will be less likely to fall asleep while feeding. If your baby is a cat napper, he may need to take a few short naps between feedings.

Activity

After eating it is important to engage your baby in some kind of activity before going back to sleep. This will further break the feeding to sleep connection. Very young babies may only be up for a short period of time before needing to go back to sleep and that is fine. An activity for a very young baby may simply be a diaper change or a brief cuddle. However, as your baby matures, he will start to have alert periods. It is during these alert periods that you can interact with him, or place him in an activity such as a bouncy seat or on an activity mat.

Sleep

A period of sleep or a nap will follow the activity period. It is important to keep one eye on your baby and one eye on the clock in order to gauge when your baby needs to return to sleep. Remember to look for signs of sleepiness. Signs of sleepiness at this age usually include yawning, turning head to side, becoming dazed, and/or fussing. Keep in mind the windows of opportunity. Most newborns can only stay awake for about forty five minutes to one hour.

(This includes time spent feeding.) As your baby grows and develops, he will be able to stay awake for longer periods of time. By the age of three months, he may even be able to stay awake for two hours.

To get your baby to be able to fall asleep on his own, you can let your baby suck on a pacifier until he is sleepy, but not totally asleep. Remove the pacifier from the baby's mouth and let him fall asleep on his own without having something in his mouth. Your baby may resist and at this time it is okay to give him back the pacifier and try again at the next sleep period. When he is drowsy but awake, gently lower him (swaddled) into his bed with his feet slightly lower than his head to avoid invoking his startle reflex. Eventually, he will learn to fall asleep without sucking. However, if your baby is sound asleep and under the age of eight weeks old, it is not necessary to wake her up to put her back to sleep. This most likely will backfire in a baby this young.

If your baby fusses when being put down drowsy but awake, it is okay to let her fuss for five minutes before falling asleep as long as you know she is not hungry, sick or has a dirty diaper. Some babies need to fuss a little in order to fall asleep and by picking them up you may be further over stimulating them and therefore cause more crying. If you cannot possibly bear to hear your baby fuss, pick up your baby and calm her and place her in her bed again when she is drowsy but awake. Continue to calm her as long as necessary. According to the American Academy of Pediatricians, some babies may actually need to let off energy by crying in order to settle to sleep or rouse themselves out of it. Five minutes of fussing won't do your child any harm as long as you make sure she's not crying out of hunger or pain, or because her diaper is wet.

If your baby is able to fall asleep on her own or with minimal assistance, then by all means, let her. If you baby becomes very agitated and needs you to comfort her to sleep, then do so. Just try not to do it every time as you do not want your baby to rely on you for help with falling asleep, especially as she nears the three to four month mark. Try to put your baby down drowsy but awake **at least** once a day during the first few months. If you have spent over twenty minutes trying to calm your fussy baby with no success, swaddle him and place him in his bed in a darkened room. He may then calm down on his own because he was over stimulated and your efforts to soothe him were making it worse.

Once your baby is asleep do not respond immediately to sleeping noises. Babies make many noises in their sleep, not always necessarily indicating that they are awake. By responding to every noise, you may inadvertently wake your baby when he was really still sleeping.

Time for you

By following the F.A.S.T. plan, you will find that your baby will become more predictable and you will now have some time for yourself. (Although you will probably spend most of your time straightening the house or taking care of other children!) Make sure that during some of these periods you also take some time to relax and recuperate, you deserve it.

Note: Some babies awaken long before it is time to feed again. If your baby wakes up more than one hour before a feeding, it is best to put your baby back to sleep before his next feeding so that he does not fall asleep while feeding. If he awakens less than an hour before feeding, than you may need to put him immediately to sleep after the feeding and try again next time. It is better to have a well-rested baby than a sleep-deprived baby.

Night feedings

Usually young infants have one long sleep period at night before waking up again to eat. As an infant grows and develops these sleep periods lengthen (i.e. four to six hours for a six-week old, six to eight hours for an eight-week old etc.). However, these long periods of sleep do not always match than of an adult. You can either choose to let your baby awaken on his own for a feeding or do a "dream feed." Some babies do better than others with dream feeds so you really need to decide for yourself. Once you pick a method make sure you be consistent and stick with. You do not want to keep switching back and forth. Should you wish to dream feed, follow the guidelines below:

Dream Feeding

Dream feeding is a method of "topping off" your baby at night without waking your baby. The dream feed usually occurs between ten or eleven p.m., before you go to bed. Since your baby is essentially asleep or very drowsy during the dream feed, your baby's sleep is uninterrupted and he will promptly return into a deep sleep after the feed.

The purpose of dream feeding is to minimize night wakings caused by hunger. But since babies usually have and need a much earlier bedtime than adults, your baby's longest sleep period often does not coincide with your bedtime.

By "topping off" or dream feeding your baby before your bedtime, the entire family gets more rest, as your baby's longest sleep period is shifted to match your sleep period. Many parents who used this technique reported that their little ones started sleeping through the night between eight to twelve weeks of age.

Dream feeding is appropriate for babies that need night feedings. Most healthy babies need one or two night feedings up to six months old. It is best start dream feeding as early as possible. It is easier to do with babies less than four months old. Older babies up to six months old, may still benefit from it, but may take longer to adjust.

How to Dream Feed

If You Are Breastfeeding:

Gently lift your sleeping baby from her crib and place her at your breast. Gently touch your baby's lips with your nipple to induce the baby to latch and suckle (usually the scent of the mother and her milk will encourage the baby to do so). In the beginning, it may take some time for a sleepy baby to latch on, particularly the younger ones.

If your baby is too sleepy to nurse properly or latch on, rouse her a little by rubbing her cheeks, lips or chest. When your baby is done, gently place her back into her crib. No burping is necessary, as little or no air is taken when your baby is very relaxed.

If You Are Bottle feeding:

Gently lift your sleeping baby from his crib and place the nipple of the bottle between the baby's lips. (This and the taste of milk will usually induce the baby to drink.) If the baby is too sleepy, gently rouse the baby a little by rubbing her cheeks or chest. No burping is necessary, as little or no air is taken in when your baby is very relaxed.

If you are just starting to dream feed, try it out for about a week. It takes time for your baby to get used to it. Initially, it may take some time for your baby to latch on or to drink from the bottle. With time, it gets much easier as your baby is conditioned to expect a feed at a particular time.

If your baby happens to wake during the dream feed, which rarely occurs, gently soothe her back to sleep. It is important not to dream feed your baby too late at night, as it may disturb his night sleep and cause night wakings. **Do not dream feed later than eleven pm**.

Your baby can be weaned from the dream feed around the third to sixth month depending on your baby's weight and pediatrician's recommendation. Weaning is done by gradually decreasing the amount of milk in the bottle or minutes nursed over a period of a week.

Some babies naturally cluster feed at night. Cluster feeding is when your baby feeds more often than usual. Cluster feeding your baby in the evening in combination with the dream feed can help lessen the amount of night wakings. (i.e. feed at six and eight p.m. before bedtime, then dream feed at ten or eleven p.m.) Cluster feeding is suitable for younger babies, usually under eight weeks old and no older than twelve weeks of age.

As your baby grows and is gaining weight steadily, you can begin to stretch the feedings so that he is eating every four hours (if he is not doing so already). This should occur around eight weeks of age. To do this, try distracting your baby by playing with him, soothing him, or offering him a pacifier. You may need to work in fifteen minute increments over a few days to get to the final goal of four hours between feedings but that's okay. Your baby will now begin taking more at each feeding, which will help him make it to the following four hour feeding.

Naps Under Four Months of Age

Napping isn't very predictable at this age. However, it is very important that your baby returns to sleep no longer than one to two hours after his last awakening. Some babies this age can only stay awake for forty five minutes before needing to return to sleep. Remember to keep one eye on the clock and one eye on your baby. This is your "window of opportunity." Look for signs of sleepiness during the day such as: decreased activity, quieting down, losing interest in people and toys (looking away), rubbing eyes, looking dazed, fussing, and/or yawning.

During the day record the time your baby wakes up and try to help her nap within one to two after waking to avoid having her becoming overtired. If your baby becomes overtired, she will not be easy to place in a bed to sleep nor will she be able to maintain sleep. Keep your nap routine simple but similar to your bedtime routine. By about four months of age, you want your baby napping in the crib for most of his naps.

If your baby has difficulty falling asleep, continue to soothe her and place her in her bed drowsy as you would at night. Do not let your baby become overtired. It will make it more difficult for her to get to sleep, make her more fussy, and disrupt her natural sleep cycle.

In addition, do not let your infant sleep longer than three to four hour blocks during the day. If he is napping longer than three or four hours, wake him up. It may take a number of months before your baby establishes a real napping schedule.

As much as it is important to instill good sleep habits from the beginning, it is not always possible. There will be times when you need to do whatever it takes to calm your baby. However, if you follow the guidelines you will find that there will be fewer times like these. If all else fails and nothing mentioned above works, swaddle your baby and place her in her bed in a dark room with a sound machine. Let her fuss for no more than five minutes. She may need this time to calm down on her own and may even fall asleep.

Overall Key Points

Remember to:

- Put your baby into the bassinet/crib at the first signs of drowsiness.
- Keep your routine as consistent as possible.
- Observe the windows of opportunity.

- Never wake a sleeping baby unless you are protecting a sleep schedule, doing a dream feed, or if the baby missed a feeding. It will disrupt their natural sleep cycle.
- Enjoy your time with your baby!

10

Babies Four Months
to Three Years

There are so many approaches to sleep coaching that it makes it difficult for exhausted new parents to choose one that is right for them. Researchers from the American Academy of Sleep Medicine have concluded "There is no single best approach for teaching your baby to sleep well. All the methods work, provided parents follow one simple rule – consistency." Families need to be able to figure out what works best for them and their children and stick with it. Being consistent in your approach to remedying your child's sleep problem as well as being on the same page as your partner and/or caregiver is the most important key to consider in sleep coaching. Remember do not start sleep coaching your baby until he is **at least** four months old **and** weighs at least fourteen pounds.

It is important to remember that no two babies are alike, so there cannot be a cookie cutter sleep program out there for all babies. In addition, your beliefs as a parent differ from beliefs as other parents. One sleep coaching method may work for one family but not for another. This book provides you with solutions to your baby's sleep problems based specifically on you and your baby's needs without having to purchase and read numerous books on baby sleep and waste precious time trying to figure them all out.

Before You Begin Sleep Coaching

Your child is having difficulty sleeping. You're exhausted and at your wits end. You are not alone. Many parents suffer by themselves through the lonely all nighters with their darling bundles of joy. The reason for this is because your child has not yet learned how to fall asleep on his own.

Before you begin sleep coaching your child you must understand two things. One, sleep is as important for your child as is a healthy diet. Two, sleep is a learned process. You must teach your child to sleep essentially by coaching him to sleep just as you teach him about good nutrition by providing him with healthy foods. If you wouldn't deprive your child of healthy foods, why would you deprive your child of sleep?

Brief awakenings throughout the night are normal. A problem arises when your baby has not yet learned the ability to put himself back to sleep by self-soothing. He will then cry out for a parent or caregiver who will do it for him as he or she did when he initially went to sleep. That's fine and dandy if you want to continue to get up and soothe your child every time he awakens throughout the night for the next ten years! But if you don't, you need to teach your child self-soothing skills and that's what I am here to show you.

Before you begin sleep coaching your baby make sure that:

❑ Your baby is four months old and weighs fourteen pounds. Most pediatricians agree that this is the age and weight when babies are able to go through a night without a feeding.

❑ Your baby is not sick.

❑ You consult your pediatrician to rule out any medical factors and advise him of any sleep changes you are going to make.

❑ You make sure that you will be able to set aside several days to sleep coaching your baby, where you will be free from distraction or any major commitments.

❑ You do not have a vacation planned within the next two weeks.

How to Wean Your Baby Off of Sleep Aids

Many parents often ask me if they should eliminate a sleep aid before or after the sleep coaching process. It is important to eliminate all sleep aids before or while sleep coaching your baby. A child must develop the ability to calm himself. This ability is essential for adapting to the environment and for his future mental health. The ability to calm oneself is essentially a learned ability in which you the parent must teach. Problems falling asleep and staying asleep are often related to the absence of the ability to self-soothe.

A sleep aid is considered anything that a baby needs use to fall asleep and cannot do it without help (i.e. parent rocking baby to sleep). The three biggest sleep aids that babies become dependent on are: motion, sucking, and swaddling. By the age of four months, it is important that you try weaning your baby off of any or all of these sleep aids as they will become detrimental to the sleep learning process.

Around the age of four months is when babies become developmentally ready to soothe themselves. If you continue to provide sleep aids, you will be robbing your baby of the ability to achieve this developmental milestone.

It is also like learning to crawl. If you always carry your baby, she'll never have the chance to discover crawling, since she would never be on the floor long enough to figure it out. When she is on the floor, you can encourage her but you cannot do it for her. She may become frustrated and cry out but you do not pick her up because you want her to be able to learn this ability. The same applies to learning to self-soothe. If you always help your baby to sleep she will never have the chance to learn how to soothe herself to sleep and will continue to awaken and cry out looking for someone to do it for her.

Motion

Between the ages of three and four months, start to gradually slow down or reduce the type of motion that your baby is relying on to sleep. For example, if your child is using the swing to sleep, gradually reduce the speed of the swing until it is not moving anymore. Once your child is able to sleep without the movement, transfer him to his bed for sleep.

If your baby is a car seat sleeper, start by placing the car seat in your baby's crib after he is asleep and have him sleep there. (Make sure you periodically check on him to make sure he is safe.) After a few days of getting used to his room, move him from the car seat into his crib.

Sucking

Sucking is probably one of the hardest sleep aids to break and therefore should be started as early as possible. You should try to use pacifiers only for soothing your baby if he is fussy. (A baby's sucking urge diminishes by six months of age, so pacifiers should be given up completely by then before it becomes a habit that will be very hard to break.)

To get your baby to be able to fall asleep on her own, you can let your baby suck until she is sleepy, but not totally asleep. Remove the bottle, breast, or pacifier from the baby's mouth and let her fall asleep on her own without something in her mouth. Your baby may resist and at this time it is okay to give her back the bottle, breast, or pacifier and start over a few minutes later when your baby once again becomes sleepy. Eventually, she will learn to fall asleep without sucking.

If your baby is used to falling asleep at the breast or during a bottle feeding, you'll have to break him or her of the need to do so. You can start by moving your child's feeding to an earlier time at night. When you see your baby starting to fall asleep during a feeding, you can temporarily discontinue the feeding and try to arouse him or her. At that point, you can then continue the feeding. Continue with this method until your baby is able to stay awake through a feeding.

Swaddling

Infants by the age of four months old no longer need to be swaddled. To transition your baby from being swaddled, start by leaving one arm out when you swaddle her. A few nights later, swaddle her with both arms out. Once your baby gets used to having her arms out, discontinue swaddling altogether. If you feel that your baby still needs a blanket to sleep, try using a wearable sleep sack, such as the HALO sleep sack.

Sound Machines

Sound machines are sleep aids, however, they are constant and do not require much effort on your part as a parent. Sound machines are okay to be used as a sleep aid throughout life. (Many adults use them to sleep.) However, if you would like to phase out the use of a sound machine, around three to four months of age, gradually lower the volume each night until the sound machine is so low that your baby no longer requires it to sleep.

The Baby Sleep Coach Sleep by Numbers Plan

Coaching your child how to sleep through the night is easy, however it does take some planning, consistency and commitment on your part. Allowing your baby to cry is not the only way to teach your baby to sleep. No matter what sleep coaching method you use, babies learn best when parents are consistent in their sleep coaching method and focus on timing and motionless sleep. Sleep coaching involves working with your child's natural sleep/wake cycles, allowing you to recognize when your baby needs to sleep, when she is exhibiting signs of drowsiness and when it's your best opportunity to get her to fall asleep. The following plan is modeled after a typical personal Baby Sleep Coach consultation.

Follow the Baby Sleep Coach's Seven Simple Steps and you will be well on your way to a good night's sleep. Gradually, your baby will begin to associate certain times of the day, some of your behaviors, his crib, and his feelings of tiredness with the process of falling asleep.

The sleep coaching process, when started at about four to six months of age, usually only takes about three days in a fairly well rested baby, and a little longer in an overtired or older baby. Depending on the sleep method chosen it may take a total of three to ten days for results. The less crying allowed in the sleep coaching process the longer it may take.

Complete the sleep method selector tool in step four and add up your points. Your total points on the sleep method selector tool will help to determine which Baby Sleep Coach method is right for you and your baby. Continue to follow the Baby Sleep Coach's Seven Simple Steps. Do NOT skip any. Once you have determined which method is right for you and your baby, go to the sleep forms in Appendix A. The first sleep form that you will find is the Bedtime Plan sleep form. Fill in this form and sign it so that you go into sleep coaching with a plan. Have your partner sign it as well and make sure you both agree on what is to be done.

The second form is the Nap time Plan sleep form. This is very similar to the Bed Time Sleep form; however this one is used for naps. Both forms are self-explanatory. If you have difficulties filling either of them out refer to the example forms also provided in Appendix B.

Next, there are the weekly sleep forms. Use the weekly forms to keep track of your baby's daily routine and progress. Refer to the example provided with weekly sleep forms for instructions on how to fill it out. You can photocopy this form so that you can continue to track your child's progress.

Lastly, there is The Baby's Sleep Coach's Sleep Rules Chart. This is used with children over the age of two. Refer to the section on sleep coaching methods for an explanation of when to use it.

Your child is having difficulty sleeping. You're exhausted and at your wits end. You are not alone. Many parents suffer through these lonely all nighters with their little bundles of joy. The reason for this is because your child has not learned how to fall asleep on his own. Babies wake up several times throughout the night. If they have not learned the ability to self-soothe then they cry out for a parent or caregiver who will do it for them as they did when they initially went to sleep. That is fine and dandy if you want to continue to get up and soothe your child every time he awakens throughout the night.

Babies enjoy the comfort of routine and consistency. If they fell asleep while being rocked in your arms, and then suddenly find themselves awake in their bed, they fully wake up and say "Hey where's my mom/dad to rock me to sleep?" Well you no longer have to continue on like this. It is your job as a parent to teach your baby that they have the ability to soothe themselves to sleep. Falling asleep is a learned skill! This is a skill that you can start teaching from birth. The earlier you start teaching your baby healthy sleep skills the better off you will be and the healthier and happier your baby will be.

Step One: Create a Sleep Environment

Preparing the Nursery

The Crib

Initially it is important to decide where your baby is going to be sleeping, whether it is in your bedroom or in his own bedroom. I would highly recommend putting your baby in his own crib in his own room. The reason why I would recommend this is because babies are not sound sleepers. The noises, gurgles, and grunts of your baby may keep you from getting quality sleep, and in addition, you may inadvertently keep your baby from getting quality sleep. In today's age, with the use of baby monitors, it is very easy to hear your baby when necessary. In addition, your baby establishes that his crib and his room are for sleeping.

Your baby's crib should be free of any stimulating toys, and the nursery should be painted in soothing pastel colors. One article that I came across actually stated that if a baby's room is painted yellow, it may make them cry more. A baby needs to know that his bedroom is for sleeping and may become over stimulated if his crib is filled with toys, mobiles, and bright colors. Plan to place your baby down to sleep in the same place for naps and bedtime.

Note: If your child is climbing out of the crib before the age of two, for their own safety, I would recommend lowering the crib to the lowest level, removing any bumpers, blankets and/or stuffed animals that may aid in his escape. If your child still manages to get out, quickly place him back in his bed and tell him it's time for sleep. Make sure you baby proof his room and add a safety gate to his doorway if necessary. Moving a child to a bed before age two doesn't solve sleep problems, it only makes them worse.

CoSleeping

Although, for safety reasons, I do not recommend cosleeping, The Baby Sleep Coach System can be used with parents who cosleep with their babies. If you choose to cosleep follow these safety tips to keep your baby safe:

❑ Your mattress should be placed on the floor to ensure safety. If your baby is at an age where he is mobile, he is more likely to fall off of a raised bed.

❑ If your bed is raised off the floor make sure that you use child safe mesh guardrails to prevent your baby from falling. In addition make sure that there is no space between the bed and guardrails where your baby can become trapped.

❑ Use extreme caution when using pillows or blankets as to avoid accidental suffocation.

❑ Never leave your baby alone in the bed unless the bed is on the floor, the room has been baby proofed, and you are able to supervise him.

❑ Do not sleep with your baby if your under the influence of alcohol or any type of drug.

Note: A review of the literature has provided

contrasting information concerning whether co-sleeping is safe. One risk associated with co-sleeping is suffocation. In addition, co-sleeping may lead to lighter infant sleep and increased night-awakenings. The U.S. Consumer Product Safety Commission (CPSC) and the American Academy of Pediatrics (AAP) warns parents not to place their infants to sleep in adult beds, stating that the practice puts babies at risk of suffocation and strangulation.

Darkness

Invest in room darkening shades to help block out any unnecessary light that may impede sleep, day or night. Darkness triggers the brain to release melatonin, a sleep hormone. It is not necessary to install a night light. Your baby is pretty accustomed to a dark environment (the womb). If your baby seems calmer with a night light or you enjoy having it in the room then it is okay to use. However, make sure that it is a dim night light.

Noise

A white noise machine or fan is also recommended as a way to block out any unnecessary environmental noise that may also impede sleep. In addition, this recreates the sound of the womb and is comforting to the baby. (Target sells them for about ten to fifteen dollars.)

Temperature

The ideal temperature for sleeping is around sixty eight to seventy two degrees Fahrenheit. A sharp drop in body temperature induces sleep, which is often why a bath is recommended before bed. Dress and cover your baby according to your own comfort level. Babies do not need more layers than adults. You can dress your baby in a light sleeper during the warmer months and a fleece sleeper during the colder months. For added warmth on colder nights, you can add an undershirt underneath. To tell if your baby is too warm or cold, feel the back of her neck or ears.

Transitional Objects

After six months of age, infants who fall asleep in the absence of their parents are more likely to use transitional objects than those who tend to fall asleep in the presence of a parent. You may leave a small, safe transitional object with your baby once he or she is over the age of six months old, can roll over, and can lift and move his or her head easily. Choose a small stuffed animal (with no removable parts) or a small breathable blanket (a twelve inch by twelve inch square will suffice) for your child. If you prefer you can sleep with it a few nights ahead of time so that it has your scent. (A mother's scent is soothing to a baby). Incorporate this object into your child's bedtime routine. For example, have your child hold it while you read books, or sing songs. Place the object in bed with your child when you put him to sleep.

Nighttime Diapers

Many parents find the super absorbent diapers made especially for nighttime to be very useful. I highly recommend using nighttime diapers once your baby reaches the size in which they are sold. It will make her feel drier at night and there will be less of a chance that a leaky diaper will awaken her. If you find that the overnight diaper is still leaking, try placing a regular diaper over it (double diapering).

Sleep Safety Tips

• Always place your baby to sleep on his or her back, even during nap time.

• Do not smoke around your baby.

• Place baby on a firm mattress in an approved crib. Avoid using an old or used crib or cradle. For the most recent safety recommendations, visit the U. S. Consumer Product Safety Commission at www.cpsc.gov.

• Make sure the mattress fits tightly to the crib or cradle without any gaps to the side.

• Remove soft, fluffy bedding and stuffed toys from

your baby's sleep area.

• Use a sleep sack instead of a blanket. If using a blanket, keep the blanket and other coverings away from your baby's mouth and nose.

• Don't overdress your baby by putting too many layers of clothing or blankets on your baby.

• Keep the bedroom at a comfortable sleeping temperature, usually about sixty-eight degrees Fahrenheit.

• Do not put your baby to sleep near a window, window blinds, cords, or curtains.

• Never tie a pacifier to your baby with a string, ribbon, or cord.

• May sure all caregivers know and follow the above tips

A word about infant sleep positioning and Sudden Infant Death Syndrome (S.I.D.S.). The American Academy of Pediatricians recommends that parents and caregivers place healthy infants on their backs when putting them down to sleep. Recent studies have shown an increased incidence of S.I.D.S. in infants who sleep on their stomachs.

Step Two: Develop a Plan

Use the weekly sleep forms located in Appendix A to document your baby's sleep and feeding schedule. Write down the time your baby fell asleep to the time your baby woke up for every nap and nighttime sleep. In addition, write down the time of each feeding and the amount. (For a breastfeeding mother, write down the amount of minutes nursed.) This will allow you to keep track of your child's total sleep, food intake, and will aid you in the sleep coaching process.

Establish a Feeding Routine

Although some people disagree, feeding and sleep do have an effect on one another. If your baby "snacks" (frequent short feedings) all day, she will not sleep as long because she will be hungry more often. Aim for at least three hours between feedings. Do not feed your baby if less than two and a half hours has passed between feedings. (Counting from the **start** of one feeding to the next.)

How to transfer nighttime feeds to the daytime:

If your baby is four months old **and** weighs fourteen pounds, he should be able to sleep through the night without a feeding. (Consult with your pediatrician first.) If your baby is still waking up to feed, you need to transfer his nighttime caloric intake into daytime (get him to take all his feedings during the day). To do this, keep track of how many ounces (or minutes nursed) your baby is taking in at night. If you are not sure of the amount of ounces (or minutes nursed) it is better to overestimate [i.e. if your baby drinks six ounces (nurses fifteen minutes) one feeding and four ounces (nurses ten minutes) the next, it is better to use the six ounces (fifteen minutes).]

When your baby awakens for a feeding, take him out of the crib (or your bed) and feed him in a chair. Give him two ounces (or nurse two minutes) less each feeding. Continue to decrease by two ounces (two minutes nursing) every other night until he is weaned off of the night feedings and is taking in all his calories during the day. Do not turn on any lights, change him only if necessary, and do not stimulate him. Try to not let him fall asleep while feeding. Remember drowsy but awake. When he is finished feeding, place him back in bed. If he cries, use the sleep coaching method that you used to put him to sleep at bedtime.

Example chart for decreasing night feedings with a bottle fed baby

Sun.	Mon.	Tues.	Wed.	Thurs.	Fri.	Sat.
6 oz.	6 oz.	4 oz.	4 oz.	2 oz.	2 oz.	0 oz.

Example chart for decreasing night feedings with a breast fed baby

Sun.	Mon.	Tues.	Wed.	Thurs.	Fri.	Sat.
10 min.	10 min.	8 min.	8 min.	6 min.	6 min.	4 min.

Establish a Bedtime

In the early evening, begin to watch your baby for signs of sleepiness (see below for examples). It is important that your baby be put to sleep before he reaches the point of exhaustion. When your baby is exhibiting signs of tiredness, do not make eye contact, it may make him more alert. Many parents mistakenly put their baby down exactly the same time every night. Parents need to be more flexible in the timing of putting their child to sleep for the night. When naps are irregular or change as your child grows, the bedtime needs to be adjusted accordingly.

Most children under the age of five need to go to bed between six thirty and seven thirty p.m. Remember, in children, later to bed does not mean later to rise. Cortisol will work against you and a cranky early riser you will have. Your baby should sleep for eleven to twelve hours a night. Do not let your child sleep past seven thirty in the morning or for more than twelve hours at night. This will cut into his daytime sleep.

If you are a working parent, you may find that your only time to play with your baby is at his or her bedtime. However, this is not the optimal situation for your baby's health. You might try putting your baby to bed at an early time and he or she will awaken happier the next morning awaiting some quality time with you before you go to work.

Signs of Sleepiness

- Decreased activity
- Quieting down
- Loses interest in people and toys
- Rubs eyes or face on shoulder or blanket
- Pulls at ears
- Looks dazed
- Fusses (often a sign that your baby is getting overtired)
- Yawns

Avoid putting your baby to bed with a pacifier. Pacifiers should only be used to satisfy your baby's need to suck. After six months of age, your baby should not need a pacifier at all. If your baby falls asleep with the pacifier, gently remove it before putting him to bed. You do not want to create a habit where you need to replace the pacifier every time your child loses it.

Step Three: Create a Bedtime Routine

You may want to try feeding your baby before a bath. Make sure the last ten to fifteen minutes of the bedtime routine are spent in the room where your child will be sleeping. Start early by establishing a bedtime routine. The half hour before bedtime is very important. Rough housing or active play will excite your child and he will have a harder time falling asleep.

Initially, your routine may only consist of a bath, changing into pajamas, and feeding. As your child gets older you can add more activities to the routine such as reading a book or singing a lullaby. However, make sure that the entire routine does not last longer than one hour (including a bath). Many parents prefer to do the bath first followed by other quiet activities.

If your child often falls asleep during a feeding, make sure then that feeding is not the last activity before bed or move your baby's bedtime earlier. In addition, it may help to lower the lights two hours before bedtime, which will allow your child's body to become aware that bedtime is approaching. Remember to keep activities calm.

You should always try to put your baby down drowsy but awake. Your baby should be quite drowsy but awake enough to know that he is going into his crib. If he falls asleep too quickly, in less than five minutes or so, you probably put him down too drowsy. Put him to bed when he's a little more alert the next night.

If your baby is still not sleeping through the night, you may need to put him to sleep a little more awake, so he gets better at soothing himself back to sleep when he awakens during a lighter stage of sleep. Even if you put him down at the right time, he might wake up a little and protest and cry as you lay him down. It's okay. Don't pick him up and start the whole routine over again. Use your sleep coaching method (from Step Four) to coach your baby to sleep.

If your baby doesn't seem to get drowsy, you should put him into his crib anyway. Make sure you carry out your bedtime routine beforehand to help him become aware that it is time for sleep. Once he's in bed, use your sleep coaching method (coming up) to help him learn to soothe himself to sleep.

Suggested Bedtime Routines

• Bath or washing hands/face
• Putting on pajamas

- Reading a story
- Wiping baby's gums / Brushing teeth
- Talking with your baby
- Saying goodnight to objects around the room
- Singing a lullaby
- Playing some quiet music
- Massage
- Feeding

Remember the bedtime routine can also be used before nap time. The routine can be shortened for nap time. For example, you can read a story and sing a lullaby before a nap. The familiar activities will relax your child and give her a cue that it is time to go to sleep.

Step Four: Choose Your Baby Sleep Coaching Method

The Baby Sleep Coach Method Selector

Use the following method selector tool to find out which sleep coaching method is right for you and your baby. For each of the following questions, pick the best answer, the statement that describes how you would feel **most of the time**.

1. Which statement do you most agree with?

  (a) Parents should adjust to their baby's lifestyle.

  (b) Babies have their own unique temperament, but parents need to provide some guidance.

  (c) Babies must be taught good sleeping habits.

2. You believe children:

  (a) are influenced by their environment and it's a parent's job to mold their personalities.

  (b) have distinctive personalities, but parents can influence how they turn out.

  (c) are influenced by their genetics and nothing can change that.

3. Your Baby's daily routine is:

  (a) somewhat regular (some set activities/routines).

(b) very regular (my baby follows a set schedule).

(c) fluctuating (everyday is different).

4. How often does your baby sleep with you?

   (a) All of the time

   (b) Sometimes

   (c) Never

5. If your baby cries in the middle of the night you:

   (a) hope the crying stops and if it continues, wait and go in after five minutes.

   (b) try to ignore it and go in after ten minutes or more.

   (c) go in immediately.

6. If a doctor asks you to administer an invasive but effective treatment to your baby for a minor medical condition, you:

> (a) refuse the treatment or question it excessively.
>
> (b) hesitate but eventually provide the treatment.
>
> (c) go ahead with it without questions.

Turn the page to add up your points and find out which sleep coaching method is right for you.

The Baby Sleep Coach Method Selector Points

Now add up the points based on your answers to the previous questions. The number of points you receive will indicate which sleep coaching method is best suited for you and your baby.

1.
   a) 1
   b) 2
   c) 3

2.
   a) 3
   b) 2
   c) 1

3.
   a) 2
   b) 3
   c) 1

4.
   a) 1
   b) 2
   c) 3

5.
   a) 2
   b) 3
   c) 1

6.

       a) 1

       b) 2

       c) 3

Total Score

If you scored 6 to 9 points turn to page 99.

If you scored 10 to 14 points turn to page 103.

If you scored 15 to 18 points turn to page 105.

The Baby Sleep Coach Methods (Step-by-Step)

The No More Tears Method (6-9 total points)

If your baby has difficulty falling asleep on his or her own, use the following method:

Positive Bedtime Routines

First: Develop a set bedtime routine of four to seven calm activities that your baby enjoys. (A list of suggested activities would include: reading books, singing a lullaby, massage, brushing teeth, talking with baby, or saying goodnight to objects around the room, etc.)

Second: Start these activities twenty minutes prior to the time your baby CURRENTLY falls asleep. Each activity is to be followed by praise and encouragement by you the parent which will then signal transition to the next activity. The total time for activities should last no longer than twenty minutes.

Third: Each night thereafter continue to carry out the same routine, however move the baby's bedtime up five to ten minutes earlier until you reach the a pre-established bedtime goal.

Fourth: If your baby cries and resists sleep following the completion of the positive routine, try soothing your baby by the side of the crib. If your baby continues to cry, pick up your baby and soothe her (without feeding) until she is calm, but not asleep. As soon as she is calm, place her back in her crib. Try not to pick her up more than once as this may further agitate her. Continue to soothe her to a calm state in her crib until she falls asleep on her own. Repeat the same key phrases every night while you are soothing her so that she begins to associate them with going to sleep. (i.e. "It's night night time.")

Fifth: As your baby gradually gets used to the sleep coaching process, begin to soothe her from further away as she falls asleep. First, start by verbally soothing her by the side of the crib, without touching her. Second, try soothing her from across the room. Lastly, try soothing her from the door. Remember to repeat your sleep key phrases. If at any time during the process, your baby becomes hysterical and you cannot calm her down, revert to what you used previously to get her to sleep, and try again the next night.

By keeping a regular, feeding, activity, and sleep schedule, you will find that your baby's internal clock becomes in tune with schedule and becomes more predictable and there will be less resistance when it comes to sleeping.

Coaching example: At nine o'clock pm, Jake's mother carried him to the bathroom where she changed his diaper and put him in his pajamas. Then she read a short story to Jake and sang him a lullaby. Lastly, she placed Jake in bed and whispered goodnight using her key sleep phrases. Jake's mother reinforced each activity by praising him. The entire routine lasted only twenty minutes. Each night, the start of the routine was moved back ten minutes in time, so that by the end of the sixth night, Jake's bedtime was eight o'clock pm. Jake cried and resisted sleep following the completion of the positive routine in the beginning, so his mother tried soothing him by the side of the crib. Jake continued to cry, so his mother picked him up and soothed him (without feeding) until he was calm, but not asleep. As soon as he was calm, she placed him back in the crib. After a few nights, as Jake's crying lessened, his mom starting verbally consoling him from the side of his bed, then from across the room, and finally by the door. Jake began to fall asleep on his own after about four weeks.

For use with night waking(s):

Scheduled Awakenings

First: Refer to the journal that you kept of your baby's sleep habits. At night, awaken your baby approximately thirty minutes before he or she would spontaneously awaken. Set an alarm clock to allow you to get up to wake your baby.

Second: Upon, awakening, provide your baby with the usual parental response as if the baby had awakened on his own.

Third: Once the spontaneous awakenings are eliminated, gradually extend the time between scheduled awakenings until your baby sleeps through the night.

Coaching example: Eva awakens at one forty-five a.m. and four-thirty a.m. every night. Her mother sets her alarm clock for one fifteen a.m. and wakes Eva. Upon awakening, she gently soothes Eva by rocking her. Eva's mother then repeats the same procedure at four fifteen a.m. Gradually as the night wakings start to disappear, Eva's mother moves the times up until Eva begins sleeping through the night.

For use with naps:

If your baby is refusing to take a nap, follow the same method above as you would if your baby was going to sleep for the night. (However, you can shorten the bed time routine.) If it has been over an hour and your baby refuses to nap, take her out of her bed and try again at the next scheduled nap time.

If you have a problem with your baby taking short naps (anything less than forty five minutes to an hour), keep track of how far into the nap your baby is awakening. Then set a timer or watch the clock and plan to sit outside her bedroom door five to ten minutes before that time. (Or watch the camera monitor if you have one.) As soon as your baby begins to stir, go in quickly and use whatever technique has worked in the past to get her to sleep. At this point, your baby should still be in a drowsy state. After about a week of using this method, your baby's naps should extend and you will longer need to intervene.

The I'll Be By Your Side Method (10-14 total points)

If your baby has trouble falling asleep on his own at night:

First: On the first night sit beside your baby's bed and **verbally** comfort and reassure him if he continues to cry. Tell him that everything is all right, that mommy/daddy is right there, and that it is time for sleep. Do not touch him.

Second: Every two days, move a little farther away from your baby. For example, move across the

room, then to the door, and then out in the hallway. If
he continues to cry and protest sleep, comfort him
quickly at five minute intervals.

If your baby awakens at night:

If he wakes up at night, during the process,
return to the position you were in when you put him
to bed (i.e. if you were seated in the chair next to him
before bed, sit in the chair again).

Coaching example: Alex's dad puts him down
to sleep at seven thirty p.m. and sits down in a chair
next to his crib. Alex starts to cry and his dad verbally
reassures Alex that he is right there. Alex continues to
cry on and off and his dad continues to verbally
assure him from the side of his bed that he is right
there. Alex eventually falls asleep, with his father at
his side.
Alex wakes up again in the middle of the night
and his father once again verbally reassures him that
he is right and it is time to sleep. After two days, his
father moves himself further from the crib. When
Alex begins to cry, his father reassures him that
everything is okay. After two more days, Alex's father
sits on a chair outside Alex's room and reassures him
from there. Alex then begins sleeping through the
night on his own.

For use with naps:

Use the same method as you would at night. However, if your baby is still awake after one hour remove him from his crib and try again for the afternoon nap. Make the afternoon nap a little earlier than normal to compensate for the missed morning nap.

The I Know You're Okay Method (15-18 total points)

First: After completing your normal bedtime routine, place your baby in bed.

Second: If your baby begins to cry, wait five minutes and go in to comfort him briefly (fifteen seconds or less). Comfort him verbally (i.e., by saying it's okay, time for sleep). Do not pick him up or touch him.

Third: Leave the room. If he continues to cry wait ten minutes before comforting him again. The goal is to wait successively longer each time before you go in. Please refer to the following chart. Use a watch/timer so you don't go back too soon. If your child becomes more angered by your presence, increase the amount of time between check ins.

Example Chart of Check ins

Day	First Wait	Second Wait	Third Wait	Add'l Waits
1	5 minutes	10 minutes	15 minutes	20 minutes
2	5 minutes	10 minutes	15 minutes	20 minutes
3	10 minutes	20 minutes	25 minutes	25 minutes
4	10 minutes	20 minutes	25 minutes	25 minutes
5	20 minutes	25 minutes	30 minutes	30 minutes

For night awakenings:

First: Wait a few minutes to make sure your baby is really awake, just not stirring. Then check on him briefly to make sure there is not a problem (i.e. wet diaper, too cold/hot, illness). Do not turn on any bright lights.

Second: Verbally comfort him for no more than fifteen seconds, but you should leave while he is still awake so that he doesn't feel you have to be present for him to fall back to sleep.

Third: Repeat the procedure every ten minutes thereafter. (Most normal full-term infants that are six months old no longer need a nighttime feeding.)

Naps

If your baby naps less than thirty minutes, try leaving him alone for an additional thirty to sixty minutes to see whether he will return to sleep unassisted. If he is crying uncontrollably for more than a few minutes or if the nap was more than thirty minutes, it is less likely that he will return to sleep. In these cases, you can try leaving him alone for an additional thirty minutes or go in and try soothing him. Although rushing in to soothe him might be counterproductive and stimulate him more.

Coaching example: Julie cries when her dad lays her down to sleep. Julie's dad waits five minutes and Julie is still crying. He goes into her room and verbally reassures her that it is okay and that it is time to sleep. He then leaves the room. Julie is still crying ten minutes later, so again he verbally reassures her that it is okay and that it is time to sleep. After fifteen minutes, Julie is still crying so he verbally reassures her that it is okay and that it is time to sleep. Finally, Julie falls asleep. However, Julie awakens at three thirty a.m. and cries. Julie's dad waits a few minutes, and goes in and verbally reassures her that everything is okay. Julie goes back to sleep. Within a few nights, Julie goes to bed on her own and sleeps through the night.

Step Five: Implement the Plan

• Start your bedtime routine twenty minutes to thirty minutes before your child's target bedtime. Allow longer if giving your baby a bath, but no more than one hour.

• Put your baby to bed super early. This means that bedtime is between six and six thirty p.m. (Trust me, it may backfire, but most likely it will not). The reason for the super early bedtime is so that your child will go to bed before he becomes overtired and will catch up on the much needed sleep he has missed. (Do not use the super early bedtime with the No More Tears method.)

• Continue to put your baby to bed between six and six thirty p.m. for three to four nights in a row.

• After four nights your baby should be caught up on sleep and can now go to bed between seven and eight o'clock. Remember to look for signs of sleepiness and base her bedtime on her napping habits and age. (i.e. if she does not take a nap one afternoon, put her to bed earlier than her usual bedtime.)

Light's Out!

Help! What do I do now?

When initially starting sleep training, you're baby will more than likely cry in protest. It is normal and it is natural. Your child is crying because it is his way of communicating. He is frustrated because he is trying to learn a new skill. If you continue to pick him up and soothe him to sleep, you are robbing him of the opportunity to learn an important life skill, how to soothe himself. Crying during sleep training will not harm or psychologically damage your baby. When you put a time limit on how much protest crying at night you can tolerate or accept before going to your baby, your teaching your baby to cry to that time limit.

It's like learning to crawl. If you always carry your baby, she'll never have the chance to discover crawling, since she would never be on the floor long enough to figure it out. When she is on the floor, you can encourage her but you cannot do it for her. She may become frustrated and cry out but you do not pick her up because you want her to be able to learn this ability. The same applies to learning to self-soothe. If you always help your baby to sleep she'll never have the chance to learn how to soothe herself to sleep.

Follow the plan as outlined above based on your customized results from The Baby Sleep Coach

Method Selector Tool. Remember you are one step closer to a full night's sleep. Stick with your plan. It will work. You should start to see results within one to three days, but complete progress usually takes one to two weeks. Your baby needs consistency. Do not stop the plan midway. He/She will get confused and it will be harder for both of you. You can do it! (Remember the No More Tears method may take up to four weeks to see results but do not give up!)

Step Six: Stick to Seven Key Components That Will Make Your Plan Work

The first and most important component to establishing a healthy sleep routine is consistency. You as a parent need to choose a method and stick with it. It may take time and patience but in the end if you are consistent in your method, it will work! Children thrive on consistency. A baby will become confused if you keep switching between several different methods. All your efforts will backfire and may even set you back farther than when you started. Be CONSISTENT.

The second key component to establishing a healthy sleep routine is predictability. Infants and toddlers thrive on predictability and routine. They like to know what is coming next and are happier when they can anticipate it. Infants and toddlers sleep and behave better when they are provided with a routine. Develop a ROUTINE and Be PREDICATBLE.

The third key component to establishing a

healthy sleep routine is communication. Communication is important both between you and your spouse, and between you and your child. Parents need to be on the same page as each other when developing, implementing, and maintaining a healthy sleep routine. You and your spouse need to communicate what you want out of the process and agree on the tactics used to achieve a healthy sleep routine. If you, as parents, are not in cooperation with each other then a healthy sleep routine will not be established and may even result in tension between you and your spouse.

In addition, from birth you need to communicate with your baby. You should narrate his day to him. For example, when getting ready for bed, you may say that it is "sleepy time". This way infants will be also be able to associate various times of the day with verbal cues. COMMUNICATE.

The fourth key component to establishing a healthy sleep routine is flexibility. It needs to be understood that a routine does not mean following a clock or a rigid schedule. A baby will most likely not wake up at the exact time, eat at the exact same time, or sleep at the exact same time every day. Most likely, a baby will stick to the same routine around similar times each day. However, there are days when the time of the routine could be a little altered and you need to "go with the flow." We as parents are not military drill sergeants and should not expect our babies to follow such a strict regimen. Be FLEXIBLE.

The fifth key component to establishing a

healthy sleep routine is establishing an early bedtime. A later bedtime does not mean a later wake up time, just as an earlier bedtime does not mean an earlier wake up time. Most babies sleep longer with an earlier bedtime. Infants are preset to go to bed early, usually around seven p.m. Putting an infant to bed late often backfires and they wake up during the night, and early the next morning. A consistent bedtime routine sets your baby's internal clock so that she is naturally sleepy at a predictable time. A consistent wake up time is as important as a regular bedtime. Babies should get up at roughly the same time every day within 30 minutes. SLEEP INDUCES SLEEP.

The sixth key component to establishing a healthy sleep routine is to try limiting the use of sleep aids (i.e., rocking, swinging, sucking, etc.) after the age of three to four months. Babies need to fall asleep on their own, not with the use of a sleep aid. Babies who become dependent on sleep aids need those aids to be in place every time they need to fall asleep. I don't know about you, but as a parent I do not want to be rocking my child to sleep each time they wake up at night, or get out of bed to retrieve a lost pacifier every time they awaken and cry out for it.

Babies who are put to sleep with these aids will look for them when they awaken in the middle of the night and cannot make use of them without your assistance. Avoid putting your baby to sleep with a pacifier. In addition, motion (i.e. swing, car, stroller) may be detrimental to your baby's sleep. Motion during sleep may keep the brain in a lighter sleep and reduce the quality and restorative effects of sleep. (Please note however that there may be a few times when only sleep aids will work in establishing sleep. It is okay to use sleep aids occasionally, but do not establish a habit of using them often.) USE AIDS ONLY FOR SOOTHING during fussy periods, NOT AS SLEEP AIDS.

Lastly, the seventh key component to establishing a healthy sleep routine is providing a baby with a blanket or stuffed toy as security. Babies often choose an object as their security object which is there for them in the night when you are not. Babies are comforted by this object and it in effect soothes them. Make sure the object is something that they are able to reach and hold onto by themselves. A word of caution however, to reduce the risk of Sudden Infant Death Syndrome it is recommended that infants do not sleep with anything in their crib. If you choose to give your child a security object before the age of one year, make sure that the object will be safe (i.e. a twelve inch by twelve inch blanket). Encourage use of a TRANSITIONAL OBJECT.

Overall Key Points

Remember to:

• Put your baby into the crib at the first signs of drowsiness.

• Keep your routine as consistent as possible.

• Observe the windows of opportunity.

• Never wake a sleeping baby unless you are protecting a sleep schedule or if the baby missed a feeding. It will disrupt their natural sleep cycle.

• Enjoy your awake time with your baby and cherish your moments alone when your baby is finally sleeping.

Step Seven: Enjoy Your Free Time and Get Some Much Needed Sleep

Make sure that you devote time for yourself to wind down and relax. Caring for a child is a strenuous task and you need to take some time for yourself. Now that your baby is sleeping, take a hot bath, read a good book, or spend time with your partner. Most importantly, SLEEP. Your body needs to catch up on some much needed sleep.

The following sleep tips will help you if you are having difficulty sleeping after months of sleep deprivation:

• Exercise during the day, at least 30 minutes three times a week. Many studies have shown that moderate, regular exercise not only reduces insomnia but also improves the quality of sleep.

• Set your body clock by keeping the same sleep schedule, seven days a week. Go to bed and wake up around the same time. Set your bedtime earlier if necessary.

• Create a comfortable sleep environment--cool, dark and uncluttered. White noise, eyeshades or ear plugs can help.

• No caffeine (including cola, chocolate) in the p.m. Avoid spicy foods. Finish eating at least three hours before bedtime

• No computers, television or arguments half an hour before bed. Soothing music and reading are good alternatives.

• If you're still awake after twenty minutes in bed, get up, go to another room and do some quiet activity. Repeat as needed.

11

Over Three Years Old
or Sleeping in a Bed

There are so many approaches to sleep coaching that it makes it difficult for exhausted parents to choose one that is right for them. Researchers from the American Academy of Sleep Medicine have concluded "There is no single best approach for teaching your child to sleep well. All the methods work, provided parents follow one simple rule – consistency."

There is not one specific sleep approach for every child. Families need to be able to figure out what works best for them and their children and stick with it. Being consistent in your approach to remedying your child's sleep problem as well as being on the same page as your partner and/or caregiver is the most important key to consider in sleep coaching.

It is important to remember that no two children are alike, so there cannot be a cookie cutter sleep program out there for all babies. In addition, your beliefs as a parent differ from beliefs of other parents. One sleep coaching method may work for one family but not for another. This book provides solutions to your child's sleep problems based specifically on you and your child's needs.

Before You Begin Sleep Coaching

Your child is having difficulty sleeping. You're exhausted and at your wits end. You are not alone. Many parents suffer by themselves through the lonely all nighters with their darling bundles of joy. The reason for this is because your child has not yet learned how to fall asleep on his own.

Before you begin sleep coaching your child you must understand two things. One, sleep is as important for your child as is a healthy diet. Two, sleep is a learned process. You must teach your child to sleep essentially by coaching him to sleep just as you teach him about good nutrition by providing him with healthy foods. If you wouldn't deprive your child of healthy foods, why would you deprive your child of sleep?

Your child naturally wakes up several times throughout the night. If he has not yet learned the ability to put himself back to sleep by self-soothing then he will cry out for or seek a parent or caregiver who will do it for him as that person did when he initially went to sleep. Children enjoy the comfort of routine and consistency. If they fell asleep while being rocked in your arms, and then suddenly found themselves awake in their bed, they fully wake up and say "Hey, where's my mom/dad to rock me to sleep?" That's fine and dandy if you want to continue to get up and soothe your child every time he awakens throughout the night. But if you don't, you need to teach your child self-soothing skills and that's what I am here to show you.

You no longer have to continue on like this. It is your job as a parent to teach your child that they have the ability to soothe themselves to sleep. Falling asleep is a learned skill! This is a skill that you can start teaching from birth. The earlier you start teaching your child healthy sleep skills the better off you will be in the end.

Before you begin sleep coaching your child make sure that:

❑ Your child is not sick.

❑ You consult your pediatrician to rule out any medical factors and advise him of any sleep changes you are going to make.

❑ You make sure that you will be able to set aside several days to sleep coaching your child, where you will be free from distraction or any major commitments.

❑ You do not have a vacation planned

❑ within the next two weeks.

How to Wean Your Child Off of Sleep Aids

Many parents often ask me if they should eliminate a sleep aid before or after the sleep coaching process. It is important to eliminate all sleep aids before or while sleep coaching your child. A child must develop the ability to calm himself. This ability is essential for adapting to the environment and for his future mental health. The ability to calm oneself is essentially a learned ability in which you the parent must teach. Problems falling asleep and staying asleep are often related to the absence of the ability to self-soothe.

A sleep aid is considered anything that a child needs to use to fall asleep and cannot do it without help (i.e. parent rocking child to sleep). Teaching your child to soothe himself to sleep is like teaching your child how to ride a bicycle. When initially teaching your child to ride a bicycle, you buy him a bicycle with training wheels. As he grows and develops, you take off the training wheels so that he can learn to balance without the aid of the training wheels. If you did not take the training wheels off, your child would not be able to learn to ride a bicycle. The same applies to sleep: If your child does not learn to soothe herself to sleep without the use of sleep aids, she will not sleep through the night.

Sucking

Sucking is probably one of the hardest sleep aids to break. If your child is used to falling asleep at the breast, during a bottle-feeding, or with a pacifier you'll have to break him or her of the need to do so. A child over the age of twenty-four months should no longer require a bottle or a pacifier. If your child is still using a bottle or a pacifier, I recommend you stop cold turkey. There is no easy way at this age to wean your child of the habit other than complete removal. If you want, you can pack up all the bottles or pacifiers with you child and have him "send them to a baby that needs them."

Rocking

Just like sucking, there is no easy way at this age to wean your child off the habit of being rocked to sleep. You may rock your child until he is in a drowsy or calm state for a few nights during the sleep coaching process. However, you may not rock him to sleep. It is important that you break him of this habit.

Sound Machines

Sound machines are sleep aids, however, they are constant and do not require much effort on your part as a parent. Sound machines are okay to be used as a sleep aid throughout life. (Many adults use them to sleep.) As your child gets older (over one year of age), you can begin to lower the volume on the sound machine so that it is not as loud as when he was an infant. However, if you would like to phase out the use of a sound machine, around three to four months of age, gradually lower the volume each night until the sound machine is so low that your baby no longer requires it to sleep.

The Baby Sleep Coach Sleep By Numbers Plan

Coaching your child how to sleep through the night is easy, however it does take some planning and commitment on your part. The following plan is modeled after a typical Private Baby Sleep Coach consultation.

Follow the Baby Sleep Coach's Seven Simple Steps and you will be well on your way to a good night's sleep. Complete the sleep method selector tool in step four and add up your points. Your total points on the sleep method selector tool will help to determine which Baby Sleep Coach method is right for you and your child. Continue to follow the Baby Sleep Coach's Seven Simple Steps. Do NOT skip any.

Once you have determined which method is right for you and your child, go to the sleep forms section in Appendix A. The first sleep form that you will find is the Bedtime Plan sleep form. Fill in this form and sign it so that you go into sleep coaching with a plan. Have your partner sign it as well and make sure you both agree on what is to be done.

The second form is the Nap Time Plan sleep form. This is very similar to the Night Time Sleep form; however this one is used for naps. Both forms are self-explanatory. If you have difficulties filling either of them out refer to the example forms in Appendix B.

Next, there are the weekly sleep forms. Use the journal forms to keep track of your child's daily routine and progress. Refer to the example in Appendix B for instructions on how to fill it out.

Lastly, there is The Baby's Sleep Coaches Sleep Rules Chart. This is used with children over the age of two. Refer to the section on sleep coaching methods for an explanation of when to use it.

Step One: Create a Sleep Environment

Setting the Sleep Stage

The Crib/Bed

Your child should have a room or space of his own to sleep in. Your child's room should be free of any stimulating toys. A child needs to know that his bedroom is for sleeping and may become over stimulated if his room is filled with toys. Plan to have your child sleep in the same place for naps and bedtime.

If your child is under the age of two and a half years old and sleeping in a bed, I highly recommend you put him back in a crib and refer to the previous chapter for a sleep coaching plan. Children under the age of two and a half do not have the cognitive ability to understand the "rules of a big bed". For safety reasons, it is also better for a child under the age of two and a half to be in a crib. The closer your child is to the age of three the better she will transition to a bed.

When purchasing a bed, it is optimal to either convert the crib to a toddler bed or use a toddler bed. Many children are comforted by the size of this bed as it is similar to their crib. If a toddler bed is not an option, then purchasing a regular size bed is fine.

CoSleeping

Although, I do not recommend cosleeping, The Baby Sleep Coach System can be used with parents who cosleep with their children. If you choose to cosleep:

- Your mattress should be placed on the floor to ensure safety. You do not want your child to accidentally fall off the bed.

- If your bed is raised off the floor make sure that you use mesh guardrails to prevent your child from falling. In addition make sure that there is no space between the bed and guardrails where your child can become trapped.

- Use extreme caution when using pillows or blankets as to avoid accidental suffocation.

- Never leave your child alone in the bed unless the bed is on the floor, the room has been child proofed, and you are able to hear him.

Darkness

In addition, invest in room darkening shades to help block out any unnecessary light that may impede sleep, day or night. Darkness triggers the brain to release melatonin, a sleep hormone. It is not necessary to install a night light. If your child seems calmer with a night light or you enjoy having it in the room then there it is okay to use. However, make sure that it is a dim night light. Make sure to open the shades in the morning as bright morning light helps regulate sleep.

Noise

A white noise machine or fan is also

recommended as a way to block out any unnecessary environmental noise that may also impede sleep. (Target sells them for about 10-15 dollars).

Temperature

The ideal temperature for sleeping is between sixty eight and seventy two degrees Fahrenheit. A sharp drop in body temperature induces sleep, which is often why a bath is recommended before bed. Dress and cover your child according to your own comfort level. Children do not need more layers than adults. You can dress your child in light pajamas during the warmer months and a fleece sleeper or flannel pajamas during the colder months. For added warmth on colder nights, you can add an undershirt underneath. To tell if your child is too warm or cold, feel the back of her neck or ears. At this age, your child may also use a blanket to sleep.

Transitional Objects

After 6 months of age, children who fall asleep in the absence of their parents are more likely to use transitional objects than those who tend to fall asleep in the presence of a parent. You may leave a small, safe transitional object with your child. Choose a small stuffed animal (with no removable parts) or a blanket for your child. If you prefer you can sleep with it a few nights ahead of time so that it has your scent. (A mother's scent is soothing to a child). Incorporate this object into your child's bedtime routine. For example, have your child hold it while you read books, or sing songs. Place the object in bed with your child when you put him to sleep.

Nighttime Diapers/Potty Training

Many parents find the super absorbent diapers made especially for nighttime to be very useful. I highly recommend using nighttime diapers or nighttime pull-ups if your child is still in diapers or has accidents at night. It will make her feel drier at night and there will be less of a chance that a leaky diaper or a wet bed will awaken her.

If your child is newly potty trained, make sure they go to the bathroom before bed. If your child requests to go to the bathroom again before bed, take them one more time to the bathroom and tell them that "that's it, it's time for bed." Some children will use the potty excuse to delay or get out of going to bed.

Step Two: Develop a Plan

Use the weekly sleep forms in Appendix A to document your child's sleep and eating schedule. Write down the time your child fell asleep to the time your child woke up for every nap and nighttime sleep. In addition, write down the time of each meal and the amount eaten. This will allow you to keep track of your child's total sleep, food intake, and will aid you in the sleep coaching process.

Establish a Bedtime

In the early evening, begin to watch your child for signs of sleepiness (see below for examples). It is important that your child be put to sleep before he reaches the point of exhaustion. Do not engage your child in any roughhousing or other physically stimulating activities one hour before bedtime. In addition, do not let your child watch television or play video games one hour before bedtime.

Most children between the ages of two and five need to go to bed between seven and eight p.m. Remember, in children later to bed does not mean later to rise. Cortisol will work against you and a cranky early riser you will have. Your child should sleep for ten to twelve hours a night. Do not let your child sleep past seven thirty in the morning or for more than twelve hours at night. This will cut into his daytime sleep.

If you are a working parent, you may find that your only time to play with your child is at his or her bedtime. However, this is not the optimal situation for your child's health. You might try putting your child to bed at an early time and he or she will awaken happier the next morning awaiting some quality time with you before you go to work.

Signs of Sleepiness

• Decreased activity
• Quieting down
• Loses interest in people and toys
• Rubs eyes/ears
• Looks dazed
• Irritable (often a sign that your child is getting overtired)
• Yawns

Step Three: Create a Bedtime Routine

Make sure the last ten to fifteen minutes of the bedtime routine are spent in the room where your child will be sleeping. Start early by establishing a bedtime routine. The half hour before bedtime is very important. Roughhousing or active play will excite your child and he will have a harder time falling asleep. Make sure that the entire routine does not last longer than one hour (including a bath). Many parents prefer to do the bath first followed by other quiet activities. In addition, it may help to lower the lights two hours before bedtime, which will allow your child's body to become aware that bedtime is approaching. Remember to keep activities calm.

Suggested Bedtime Routines

• Bathing or washing hands/face

- Putting on pajamas
- Reading a story
- Brushing teeth
- Talking with your child
- Saying goodnight to objects around the room
- Singing a lullaby
- Playing some quiet music

Step Four: Choose Your Baby Sleep Coaching Method

The Baby Sleep Coach Method Selector

Use the following method selector tool to find out which sleep coaching method is right for you and your child. For each of the following questions, pick the best answer, the statement that describes how you would feel **most of the time**.

1. Which statement do you most agree with?

    (a) Parents should adjust to their baby's lifestyle.

    (b) Babies have their own unique temperament, but parents need to provide some guidance.

    (c) Babies Must be taught good sleeping habits.

2. You believe children:

    (a) are influenced by their environment and it's a parent's job to mold their personalities.

    (b) have distinctive personalities, but parents can influence how they turn out.

    (c) are influenced by their genetics and nothing can change that.

3. Your child's daily routine is:

    (a) somewhat regular (some set activities/routines).

    (b) very regular (my baby follows a set schedule.

    (c) fluctuating (everyday is different).

4. How often does your child sleep with you?

    (a) All of the time

    (b) Sometimes

(c) Never

5. If your child cries in the middle of the night you:

    (a) hope the crying stops and if it continues, wait and go in after five minutes.

    (b) try to ignore it and go in after ten minutes or more.

    (c) go in immediately

6. If a doctor asks you to administer an invasive but effective treatment to your child for a minor medical condition, you:

    (a) refuse the treatment or question it excessively.

    (b) hesitate but eventually provide the treatment.

    (c) go ahead with it without questions.

Turn the page to add up your points and find out which sleep coaching method is right for you.

The Baby Sleep Coach Method Selector Points

Now add up the points based on your answers to the previous questions. The number of points you receive will indicate which sleep coaching method is best suited for you and your child.

1.

    a) 1
    b) 2
    c) 3

2.

    a) 3
    b) 2
    c) 1

3.

    a) 2
    b) 3
    c) 1

4.

    a) 1
    b) 2
    c) 3

5.

    a) 2
    b) 3
    c) 1

6.

    a) 1

    b) 2

    c) 3

Total Score

If you scored 6 to 9 points turn to page 134.

If you scored 10 to 14 points turn to page 136.

If you scored 15 to 18 points turn to page 137.

The Baby Sleep Coach Methods (Step-by-Step)

The No More Tears Method (6-9 total points)

You can ensure that your child will go to bed at night with no problem by teaching him self-quieting skills while he is awake. Engage your child in "quiet time" during certain periods of the day (i.e. reading books). During this "quiet time" she will have a chance to calm down and practice self-relaxation skills. In contrast, it is also important that your child gets an adequate amount of exercise throughout the day to ensure that she is tired at bedtime. Finally, it is important that you get your child up at the same time every day.

First: With your child, develop a set of sleep rules for a sleep chart. The rules may include brushing his teeth, putting his pajamas on, going to bed without arguing, and staying in bed once he says goodnight.

Second: Construct a sleep rules chart with positive reinforcement. You may want to create it on the computer and print it out on a piece of paper to hang on the refrigerator or be creative and make a chart out of construction paper and art supplies.

Third: Establish a long-term reward for following the sleep rules (i.e. ice cream, trip to the movies).

Fourth: After the rules have been established, hang the chart in a place where it is visible. Award a sticker or stamp the morning after each night your child successfully follows the sleep rules.

Fifth: At the end of the week if your child has followed the sleep rules successfully for four or five out of the seven days, praise and reward her with your previously established long-term reward.

Coaching example: Sally and her mom create a sleep rules chart and buy shiny gold stickers to place on it when she follows the set of sleep rules that were decided on. Sally chose a trip to the movies as her long term reward. She helps her mother hang it in the bathroom where she can see it every night. Sally gets a gold star on her chart each night she brushes her teeth, gets washed, gets dressed for bed, and stays in bed. After five nights of stars, Sally gets to go to the movies.

You can add a place on the chart for naps as well as night wakings and carry out the same method for dealing with both. You may want to keep the charts separate though as day time sleep may be a little harder to solve than night.

The I'll Be By Your Side Method (10-14 total points)

First: Create a "bedtime pass". A bedtime pass is simply an index card with your child's name written on top.

Second: The bedtime pass can be exchanged without penalty for one short visit outside the bedroom per evening and then is given to the parent for the remainder of the evening. (A timer can be used to measure the length of time out of bed.)

Third: Put a digital alarm clock in your child's room. Set the clock for a desired (reasonable) wake up time. (You can also use one of the clocks on the market now that change colors or switch pictures when it is time to get up.) Explain to your child that when the music comes on,(clock changes color, picture changes, etc.), it is time to get up and leave his room. If your child leaves his room for any reason between the bedtime pass and the morning, walk him back to his room without making eye contact or without communication.

Coaching example: Lola has difficulty staying in her bed while going to sleep at night and gets out of bed really early in the morning. Her mother creates an index card with her name on it (the bedtime pass) and tells her that she can use her bedtime pass to come out of her room one time. In addition, Lola's mom puts a color changing alarm clock on Lola's nightstand and instructs her that she must stay in her room until the clock turns green. On the first night, Lola goes to bed and comes out within 5 minutes. Her mother then instructs her that she no longer has a pass and must stay in her bed. Lola comes out six additional times and her mother brings her back to her room without making any eye contact or communicating. Lola then stays in her room all night and but comes out before the clock turns green the next morning. Lola's mom tells her that she must stay in her room until the clock turns green and shows her the clock when it turns green. Before bed the following night, Lola's mom reminds her of this rule. The next morning, Lola stays in her bed and comes out when the clock turns green exclaiming "the clock is green!" Lola's mom praises her for doing so.

The I Know You're Okay Method (15-18 total points)

First: If your child gets out of bed after his bedtime routine or at night for any other reason then to use the toilet, return him quickly to his bedroom without talking to him or making eye contact with him. Consider installing a safety gate in his doorway if necessary.

Second: If he stands at the gate, tell him you must close the bedroom door, but that you will open it in a minute when he returns to bed.

Third: If he does, open the door. If he doesn't or if he tries to open the door, hold it closed. If the screaming and pounding continue, open the door every ten to fifteen minutes, stating very quickly that you will keep it open if he lies down quietly. This allows him to learn that he is in control of whether the door is open or closed and that he must remain in his bed. (If you need to, turn the door knob backwards so that you can lock the door from the outside when necessary. Just remember to unlock it when through because it is a safety hazard to keep a young child locked in his room all night.)

Naps: Use the above method for naps as well. If your child has not fallen asleep after one hour, take your child out of his room and try again at the next nap time. If your child only takes one nap a day, plan for an earlier bedtime that evening to compensate for the loss of the nap.

Night Waking: If your child awakens in the middle of the night, briskly return him to his room without speaking with him at all. If he continues to come out, continue walking him back to his room in this manner. It may be difficult but as long as you are consistent, he will no longer get out of his bed at night.

Coaching example: Jack gets out of his bed after his mother puts him to bed for the night. Jack's mother walks him back to his room with no verbal interaction or eye contact and closes the gate at his door. Jack stands at the gate and yells for his mother. Jack's mother comes to the door and tells him that she is closing his door until he returns to his bed. Jack continues to scream and pound on the door. Five minutes later, Jack's mom opens the door and explains to him that she will keep it open if he stays in bed. Jack returns to his bed and his mother opens the door. After several times of repeating this behavior, Jack stays in his bed and falls asleep.

Step Five: Implement the Plan

• Start your bedtime routine twenty minutes to thirty minutes before your child's target bedtime. Allow longer if giving your child a bath, but no more than one hour.

• Put your child to bed super early. This means that bedtime is between six-thirty and seven. (Trust me, it may backfire, but most likely it will not). The reason for the super early bedtime is so that your child will go to bed before he becomes overtired and will catch up on the much needed sleep he has missed. (Do not do this if you are using the "No More Tears Method."

• Continue to put your child to bed between six-thirty and seven for three to four nights in a row.

• After four nights your child should be caught up on sleep and can now go to bed between seven and eight o'clock. Remember to look for signs of sleepiness and base her bedtime on her napping habits and age. (i.e. if she does not take a nap one afternoon, put her to bed earlier than her usual bedtime.)

Light's Out!

Help! What do I do now?

When initially starting sleep training, you're child will more than likely cry in protest. It is normal and it is natural. Your child is crying because it is his way of communicating. He is frustrated because he is trying to learn a new skill. If you continue to pick him up and soothe him to sleep, you are robbing him of the opportunity to learn an important life skill, how to soothe himself. Crying during sleep training will not harm or psychologically damage your child.

It is like learning to ride a bicycle. When initially teaching your child to ride a bicycle, you buy him a bicycle with training wheels. As they grow and develop, you take off the training wheels so that they can learn to balance without the aid of the training wheels. If you did not take the training wheels off, your child would not be able to learn to ride a bicycle. The same applies to sleep: If your child does not learn to soothe herself to sleep without the use of sleep aids, she will not sleep through the night.

Follow the plan as outlined above based on your customized results from The Baby Sleep Coach Method Selector. Remember you are one step closer to a full night's sleep. Stick with your plan. It will work.

You should start to see results within one to three days, but complete progress usually takes one to two weeks. Your child needs consistency. Do not stop the plan midway. He/She will get confused and it will be harder for both of you. You can do it!

Step Six: Stick to Seven Key Components That Will Make Your Plan Work

The first and most important component to establishing a healthy sleep routine is consistency. You as a parent need to choose a method and stick with it. It may take time and patience but in the end if you are consistent in your method, it will work! Children thrive on consistency. Your child will become confused if you keep switching between several different methods. All your efforts will backfire and may even set you back farther than when you started. Be CONSISTENT.

The second key component to establishing a healthy sleep routine is predictability. Toddlers thrive on predictability and routine. They like to know what is coming next and are happier when they can anticipate it. Toddlers sleep and behave better when they are provided with a routine. Develop a ROUTINE and Be PREDICATBLE.

The third key component to establishing a healthy sleep routine is communication. Communication is important both between you and your spouse, and between you and your child. Parents need to be on the same page as each other when developing, implementing, and maintaining a healthy sleep routine. You and your spouse need to communicate what you want out of the process and agree on the tactics used to achieve a healthy sleep routine. If you, as parents, are not in cooperation with each other then a healthy sleep routine will not be established and may even result in tension between you and your spouse.

In addition, from birth you need to communicate with your child. You should narrate his day to them. For example, when getting ready for bed, you may say that it is "sleepy time". This way your child will be also be able to associate various times of the day with verbal cues. COMMUNICATE.

The fourth key component to establishing a healthy sleep routine is flexibility. It needs to be understood that a routine does not mean following a clock or a rigid schedule. Your child will most likely not wake up at the exact time, eat at the exact same time, or sleep at the exact same time every day. Most likely, your child will stick to the same routine around similar times each day. However, there are days when the time of the routine could be a little altered and you need to "go with the flow." We as parents are not military drill sergeants and should not expect our children to follow such a strict regimen. Be FLEXIBLE.

The fifth key component to establishing a healthy sleep routine is establishing an early bedtime. A later bedtime does not mean a later wake up time, just as an earlier bedtime does not mean an earlier wake up time. Most children sleep longer with an earlier bedtime. Children are preset to go to bed early, usually around seven p.m. Putting a child to bed late often backfires and they wake up during night, and early the next morning. A consistent bedtime routine sets your child's internal clock so that she is naturally sleepy at a predictable time. A consistent wake up time is as important as a regular bedtime. Children should get up at roughly the same time every day within 30 minutes. SLEEP INDUCES SLEEP.

The sixth key component to establishing a healthy sleep routine is to discontinue the use of sleep aids (i.e., rocking, swinging, sucking, etc.). Children need to fall asleep on their own, not with the use of a sleep aid. Children who become dependent on sleep aids need those aids to be in place every time they need to fall asleep. I don't know about you, but as a parent I do not want to be rocking my child to sleep each time he wakes up at night, or get out of bed to retrieve a lost pacifier every time he awakens and cries out for it.

Children who are put to sleep with these aids will look for them when they awaken in the middle of the night and cannot make use of them without your assistance. Avoid putting your child to sleep with a pacifier. In addition, motion (i.e. rocking, car, stroller) may be detrimental to your child's sleep. Motion during sleep may keep the brain in a lighter sleep and reduce the quality of sleep and the restorative effects of sleep. NO SLEEP AIDS.

Lastly, the seventh key component to establishing a healthy sleep routine is providing your child with a blanket or stuffed toy as security. Children often choose an object as their security object which is there for them in the night when you are not. Children are comforted by this object and it in effect soothes them. Encourage use of a TRANSITIONAL OBJECT.

Overall Key Points

Remember to:

• Put your child to bed at the first signs of drowsiness.

• Keep your routine as consistent as possible.

• Observe the window of opportunity.

• Never wake a sleeping child unless you are protecting a sleep schedule. It will disrupt their natural sleep cycle.

• Enjoy your awake time with your child and cherish your moments alone when your child is finally sleeping.

Step Seven: Enjoy Your Free Time and Get Some Much Needed Sleep

Make sure that you devote time for yourself to wind

down and relax. Caring for a child is a strenuous task and you need to take some time for yourself. Now that your child is sleeping, take a hot bath, read a good book, or spend time with your partner. Most importantly, SLEEP. Your body needs to catch up on some much needed sleep.

The following sleep tips will help you if you are having difficulty sleeping after months of sleep deprivation:

• Exercise during the day, at least 30 minutes three times a week. Many studies have shown that moderate, regular exercise not only reduces insomnia but also improves the quality of sleep.

• Set your body clock by keeping the same sleep schedule, seven days a week. Go to bed and wake up around the same time. Set your bedtime earlier if necessary.

• Create a comfortable sleep environment--cool, dark and uncluttered. White noise, eyeshades or ear plugs can help.

• No caffeine (including cola, chocolate) in the p.m. Avoid spicy foods. Finish eating at least three hours before bedtime

• No computers, TV or arguments half an hour before bed. Soothing music and reading are good alternatives.

• If you're still awake after twenty minutes in bed, get up, go to another room and do some quiet activity. Repeat as needed.

12

Twins, Triplets, Etc.

Having more than one baby is more fun but also more work, especially when it comes to getting them to sleep! The Baby Sleep Coach System can be used with twins, triplets or more. Go to section ten or eleven, depending on your baby's age and use the Baby Sleep Coach Method Selector tool to decide on which method is best for you and your babies. Next incorporate the recommendations below to help when implementing the program:

1. Make sure your babies are sleeping in separate beds. It is okay to have them share a bed when they are first born. After the age of four months, however, they will become more active and begin to develop their own distinct sleep patterns and will disturb each other if kept in the same bed.

2. Synchronize their eating and sleeping schedules. It is okay to wake one baby to keep her on the same feeding schedule as her sibling(s).

3. Temporarily separate your babies during the sleep coaching process. If you can relocate the better sleeper to a different room. Make sure that this room is similar to their bedroom in that it is dark, away from living areas, and comfortable. You can temporarily place this baby to sleep in a portable bed such as a pack and play if necessary. This way, during the sleep coaching process, one baby will not disturb the other. Once, the babies are sleeping better, it is okay to move them back to the same room.

4. If you have the help of another adult, you can sleep coach both (all) the babies at the same time. Create a sleep coaching team. Enlist the help of friends and/or relatives and make sure everyone is on the same page. However, if you are the only one available at night to implement the sleep coaching plan than you may want to do one baby at a time.

5. When placing the babies back in the same room to sleep put a white noise machine in between the babies cribs in order to drown out any sounds and to help prevent one baby from waking the other(s). If possible, put up a curtain or divider to minimize any interaction between the babies during sleeping.

6. I highly recommend placing the babies in different rooms for naps during the day. It is hard enough

7. for babies to transition from play to sleep during the day on their own. It is even harder when you have a "pal" who wants to play. Maybe put one in your bedroom for a nap (as long as you are not in there). If that is not possible and you must keep them together, place a curtain divider as mentioned above.

8. Keep an individual sleep coaching journal for **EACH** baby separately. (See Appendix A.)

13

Frequently Asked Questions

Developmental Milestones

My newborn appears to have his days and nights confused. How do I teach him the difference?

First off, make sure that you keep your baby's room and your house well lit during the day and dimly lit at night. Make sure you wake up your baby for each scheduled feeding throughout the day when necessary. Play with him during the day and keep interactions at night to a minimum. Do not socially interact or play with your baby at night. Eventually, your baby will learn the difference between day and night.

My son is 5 months old and rolls over to his tummy when sleeping. What should I do?

Start out at night by placing your son on his back to sleep. If he is developmentally able to roll over and lift his head, it should be okay for him to sleep on his stomach if he put himself there in the first place. There should be no need for you as a parent to have to go into your baby's room all night and roll him back over, unless otherwise advised by your pediatrician. However, make sure that there are no loose blankets or stuffed toys in his crib that could jeopardize his safety.

My nine month old stands up in the crib every time I put him down for a nap. He then cannot get himself down and cries. What should I do?

Throughout the day when your baby pulls himself up on furniture or toys, sit with him and show him how to get down. Lower him down by bending him at the knees. This will allow for him to practice getting down from a standing position while out of his crib. If he continues to stand in his crib and cries because he cannot get himself down, then go in once and show him how to get down in his crib. Try not to repeat the procedure of going into him in his crib because it may lead to him crying for your attention, which in turn will lead to other sleep issues.

My baby is cutting a tooth and is waking up crying throughout the night?

The first teeth often appear around six months of age, but there is a wide range of normal for this process. Some babies start teething as early as three or four months, others do not start until twelve months.

Between six and ten months is usually considered "normal".

Although your baby may experience short periods of pain or discomfort throughout the teething process, it should not be enough to disrupt his sleep schedule. When the tooth is actively cutting through the gum, your child may experience more discomfort and this may disrupt his sleep. If your child is cutting a tooth, his gums will look red, translucent, and/or swollen. However, as soon as the tooth cuts through the gum, your child's sleep should return to normal.

During this period of time, you can offer your baby extra soothing to sleep. In addition, you (with your doctor's supervision) can offer your child some pain medication. Lastly, do not start sleep training until the teething episode has passed.

My eleven month old wants me to hold him often and cries when I put him down for bed at night?

Babies can show signs of separation anxiety as early as six or seven months, but it usually becomes most prominent between the ages of twelve to eighteen months. Your baby is at the age where he is beginning to realize he is his own person. As much as he wants to adventure out on his own, he also wants to keep you close by. Most commonly, separation anxiety strikes when you or your spouse leaves your child to go to work or run an errand. Babies can also experience separation anxiety at night. Sometimes this interferes with putting your baby to bed. There are some things you can do to help your child transition through this time of increasing individuation from you.

Start by spending a little extra time with your baby before nap and bedtime. Adding five to fifteen minutes will suffice. During this time, give him extra attention, cuddles, story time and kisses. This will allow him to see that you are there for him as well as help settle him for bed. Also give your child a transition object, such as a blanket or a stuffed toy, and incorporate it into your bedtime routine.

In addition, during his wake time play lots of games that allow your child to learn the concept of object permanence. Activities that are good for teaching object permanence are peek-a-boo, hiding a toy under a blanket or behind an object, or playing with a jack in the box.

Lastly, always say "goodbye" to your child when you are leaving her. Even if your baby cries when you leave, it is important to say goodbye because it will teach her that when you leave her you will come back. This will help lessen the anxiety and your baby will not become upset if she looks to find you.

Will starting solid foods affect my baby's sleep?

Starting solids could affect your baby's sleep if he becomes gassy, has a bad reaction, or develops an allergy to the food. With that being said, to head off any sleep issues stemming from the introduction of solid foods, always follow your pediatrician's recommendations for starting solids and always start a new food in the morning so that you have the day to see if there is a reaction. Lastly, you may want to hold off on introducing any new foods while sleep coaching so that you do not wonder if your baby's crying is due to discomfort as opposed to resistance to the sleep training.

How do I eliminate the bottle before bed?

You should plan to eliminate the bedtime bottle between the ages of twelve to fifteen months. When doing so, try incorporating a cup of water into your bedtime routine to transition your child from the bottle. You can try letting your baby hold the cup of water while you read her a book. She may protest at first but the longer you wait the harder it will become. Never put your baby to bed with a bottle.

How and when should I transition my toddler to a bed?

Plan on moving your child to a bed around the age of three. If your child is climbing out of the crib before the age of two and a half, for his safety, I would lower the crib to the lowest setting and remove all bumpers, blankets and/or stuffed toys that can be used as props to get out. You can put pillows on the floor around the crib to protect your child if he jumps out.

Keep an eye or an ear on him (by using the video or sound monitor) when putting him to bed. If he continues to jump out of bed, go into his room and place him back into his bed, without interacting with him. In a causal tone, simply tell him it's time to sleep and walk away. Continue to place him back into bed until he stops the behavior. It may take several times of placing him back in his bed but he will eventually learn and stop jumping out.

Make sure his bedroom is fully child proofed and install a safety gate in his door if necessary. Moving a child to a bed before the age of three does not solve sleep problems, it only makes them worse.

As long as your child is not endangering himself by climbing out of the crib, the longer you wait the better the transition will be. Children over the age of two and a half have better developed cognitive skills that enable them to understand the "rules" of sleeping in a big bed. I highly recommend waiting until the age of three to transition your child to a bed.

When you do transition your child to a bed, involve your child in the process. Take your child to the store with you when pick out a new bed. However, do not overwhelm him with many choices. You may want to do a preliminary search without your child and then bring him to the store with you and let him choose between two bed choices.

In addition, let him pick out special sheets for his bed. Getting him involved in the process will get him more excited and interested in making the switch to a big bed. Finally, you may want to have a special get together where your child invites a few special friends or family members for a "big bed party." Make them proud of their new transition.

My child is newly potty trained and is repeatedly asking to go to the bathroom after I put him to bed. What can I do?

Night time dryness often takes longer to master than day time dryness. It is okay and I highly recommend that you use a diaper or pull up specially made for the night time when putting your child to bed and/or nap. Also, limit your child's intake of liquids after dinner time and only allow him a small cup of water when brushing his teeth. Make sure your child uses the potty right before bedtime and teach her how to go if she needs to go at night. (It may be helpful to leave a night light on in the bathroom and/or hallway.)

Lastly, watch for the limit testing at bedtime that comes along with your newly trained child. If your child tells you he needs to go potty after he has been tucked in for the night, tell him you'll take him one time and then that is it until the morning. If he protests after that, use your sleep coaching method.

What is the difference between nighttime fears,
nightmares and night terrors?

Nighttime fears and nightmares are not uncommon and are a part of normal child development. Nightmares are thought to be most common between the ages of three and five years old. Nighttime fears are normal and also usually occur between the ages of three and five. Children may express their fear of the dark, monsters under their bed or in the closet, or of spiders, noises, etc. However, fears and nightmares can have a great impact on your child's sleep and also on the family.

Nightmares and night terrors are two different types of occurrences and should be responded to appropriately. Nightmares are when your child has a bad dream which causes him to awaken in a state of fear. He may cry out for you.

If your child wakes up at night startled from a dream, briefly comfort him in his OWN bed, if necessary. If it appears, that your child is using fear as a way to get out of going to bed or staying in bed refer back to the Baby Sleep Coach methods you had been using previously.

Night terrors are characterized by partial awakening accompanied by crying or other extreme expressions of distress. The child is typically unaware of his surroundings and parental attempts to soothe the child often fail. Night terrors appear during the first year of life and typically disappear as the child grows. Night terrors are often a consequence of insufficient sleep.

In this situation, it is best to wait for the night terror to end. If the episode continues more than five minutes, you can wake your child, and put him back to sleep once he calms down. Your child will awaken with no memory of the event in the morning.

It is important that you as a parent help your children through these periods without impacting their previously established sleep routines. Don't overreact.

Be sure not to dismiss their fears or ridicule them for feeling the way they do. Allow them to express their fears or describe their nightmares. Then as the parent show them why they have no reason to be afraid. For example, if your child is scared of a monster in their closet, open their closet with them and show them that there is no monster.

My four year old wets his bed several times a week. Is this normal? What can I do?

Five to seven million children in the United States wet the bed. There are several things that can cause bedwetting. Heredity and maturation can both play a role in why a child is wetting the bed. Some children wet the bed simply because their bladder has not grown as fast as the rest of their body. It is important to remember that children do not wet the bed on purpose.

When your child has a bed wetting accident do

not scold him or her for it. Clean it up as quickly as you can and place your child back in his or her bed and say goodnight. Let them know that it was an accident and that it is okay. Do not make a big deal of it or you may create unwanted sleep problems. It might be helpful to buy two of the protective sheet covers or double sheeting (putting on two fitted sheets and waterproof covers) your child's bed for faster changing in the middle of the night. You can also purchase a protective cover, that covers the area under your child's bottom half, that can be changed quickly in the middle of the night. Stores even sell disposables versions of these.

In addition, limit the intake of fluids two hours before bedtime and make sure your child uses the bathroom right before bedtime. If the accidents happen often, consider having your child wear pull-ups to bed. Many companies now sell them and create them to look like underwear. Lastly, make sure that you leave a nightlight on in the hallway and bathroom so that your child can safely and easily get to the bathroom in the middle of the night if need be.

Consult your pediatrician for further help or to rule out any medical conditions, if necessary. There are some devices on the market now that can be used to wake the child at the first sign of an accident but these may not be necessary.

*I recently had a baby and my three year
old is starting to wake at night again.
Why is this happening?*

Upon the arrival of a new baby, your older
child(ren) may have a little difficulty adjusting and
may experience some regression in their behavior.
During this time your older child may also wake up
at night because he hears the new baby. Explain to
him or her that "because the baby is little and has a
little tummy, he or she needs to wake up at night to
eat. Soon the baby will no longer need to eat at night
and will sleep through the night just like you."

It is important that you return your older child
to his or her bed promptly and refrain from giving
any unnecessary attention during the night. You do
not want to accidentally reinforce their new night
waking by either playing with them or scolding them
for the behavior. If necessary, use a sound machine in
your older child's room if you are not using one
already.

During The Sleep Coaching Process

*How can I get my daughter to fall asleep without
nursing/sucking?*

To get your baby to be able to fall asleep on her
own, you can let her suck until she is sleepy, but not
totally asleep. Remove the bottle, breast, or pacifier
from your baby's mouth and let her fall asleep on her

own without something in her mouth. Your baby may resist and at this time it is okay to give her back the bottle, breast, or pacifier and start over a few minutes later when she once again becomes sleepy. Eventually, she will learn to fall asleep without sucking.

When should I move my baby from bassinet to crib?

The best time to move your baby to a crib is by three months of age. To ease in the transition you may want to start by placing your baby to sleep in her bassinet in her room for a week, if she isn't there already. Next, you can start by having her nap in it once a twice a day for a few days before making the transition at night.

My baby only naps for thirty minutes at a time (catnaps). How can I lengthen her naps?

First of all, make sure that you are putting your baby down at the right time. If you put your baby down too early, she may just catnap. If you put your baby down too late, she may be overtired and not sleep well. Make sure your baby's napping environment is appropriate. The napping environment must be quiet (besides a noise machine) and comfortable, away from everyday noises and distractions.

Babies nap best where they sleep at night. Make sure that you are not rocking or soothing your baby to sleep because she may be unable to soothe herself back to sleep. If your baby begins to arouse a half an hour after falling asleep, you can try and gently pat her to get her back to sleep before she fully awakens. However, if your baby is waking up happy and appears to be well rested then there is not much you can do. If your baby is young (under five months), her naps will begin to lengthen as she gets older. Just be sure to be consistent, and observe the windows of opportunity.

My baby will only sleep in the swing or carseat. How can I transition him to his crib?

Start by moving the carseat or swing to your baby's room and have him sleep there. (Make sure you periodically check on him to make sure he is safe.) If he is in his carseat, place the carseat in the crib. If he is in the swing, gradually slow the swinging motion over a couple of days until it is totally motionless. After a few days of getting used to his room, move him from the swing or carseat into his crib.

My baby will only sleep when swaddled. How do I transition her from being swaddled?

Infants by the age of four months old no longer need to be swaddled. To transition your baby from being swaddled, start by leaving one arm out when you swaddle her. A few nights later, swaddle her with both arms out. Once your baby gets used to having her arms out, discontinue swaddling altogether.

My son is an early riser.
How can I get him to sleep later?

First of all, install room darkening shades and a sound machine if you do not already have one. Next, you need to determine if your baby is getting enough sleep at night and that he is not just an early riser. Some babies get all the sleep they need and are just naturally early risers. There is not much a parent can do about this.

However, if your baby is not getting the recommended amount of sleep for his age or he is waking up cranky in the morning, there are a few things you can try. If a leaking diaper is the problem, try using diapers especially made for nighttime. If he requires your presence to fall asleep at bedtime, he may not be able to put himself back to sleep after an early arousal in the morning.

Make sure that he is not going to bed too late. If your baby is going to bed too late, he will have more trouble sleeping soundly through the night. An earlier bedtime usually means a later wake up time.

Lastly, if your baby or toddler is already going to bed early (before seven thirty), try adjusting the bedtime later by fifteen minutes for a few nights and see if that makes a difference. For example, for a toddler, who needs an average of eleven hours of sleep, may be getting up early because he already met his night's requirement and no longer needs to sleep.

How do I deal with age appropriate nap schedule shifts/changes?

During the time when a baby transitions from three to two naps, and from two to one nap, it is important that you go with the flow. For example, when a baby gives up his third nap, it may be necessary to move up his bedtime twenty to thirty minutes earlier for a few weeks to accommodate for the absence of the third nap.

When a baby transitions from two naps to one nap, you need to move his morning nap a little later so that it turns into a middle of the day nap. In addition, you may need to put him to bed twenty to thirty minutes earlier to accommodate for this change. There also may be days during the transition period when your baby will revert back to two naps and that is okay.

My child was doing so well and two weeks after sleep coaching he started crying at bedtime again. Is everything I accomplished ruined?

Your baby is experiencing what is known in the scientific and psychological world as an extinction burst. This is when the behavior that you worked so hard to get rid of all of a sudden shows up again. It can occur at any time during the sleep coaching process. But don't worry that all you've worked so hard for is lost. Be consistent and stick with your sleep coaching method and this episode will pass shortly (usually within one night).

My baby is climbing out of the crib after I put him to bed. Should I move him to a toddler bed?

If your child is climbing out of the crib before the age of two and a half, for his safety, I would lower the crib to the lowest setting and remove all bumpers, blankets and/or stuffed toys that can be used as props to get out. You can put pillows on the floor around the crib to protect your child if he jumps out.

Keep an eye or an ear on him (by using the video or sound monitor) when putting him to bed. If he continues to jump out of bed, go into his room and place him back into his bed, without interacting with him. In a causal tone, simply tell him it's time to sleep and walk away. Continue to place him back into bed until he stops the behavior. It may take several times of placing him back in his bed but he will eventually learn and stop jumping out.

Make sure his bedroom is fully child proofed and install a safety gate in his door if necessary. Moving a child to a bed before the age of three does not solve sleep problems, it only makes them worse.

As long as your child is not endangering himself by climbing out of the crib, the longer you wait the better the transition will be. Children over the age of two and a half have better developed cognitive skills that enable them to understand the "rules" of sleeping in a big bed. I highly recommend waiting until the age of three to transition your child to a bed.

I have successfully sleep coached my baby to sleep through the night but she still continues to cry for ten to fifteen minutes when I place her down to sleep. Why is she still crying?

It is normal for some babies to cry for ten to fifteen minutes to settle themselves to sleep. It is just a way for babies to let off steam. You can think of it as equivalent to an adult thinking about things in his head before nodding off to sleep. You can try placing your baby to bed about fifteen minutes earlier than usual and see if the crying stops. If it does than you were placing your baby to bed too late.

What age should I move my child to a bed?

Plan on moving your child to a bed around the age of three. As long as your child is not endangering himself by climbing out of the crib, the longer you wait the better the transition will be. Children over the age of two and a half have better developed cognitive skills that enable them to understand the "rules" of sleeping in a big bed. I highly recommend waiting until the age of three to transition your child to a bed. (If your child is climbing out of the crib see the previous frequently asked questions involving this matter.)

When you do transition your child to a bed, involve your child in the process. Take your child to the store with you when pick out a new bed. However, do not overwhelm him with many choices. You may want to do a preliminary search without your child and then bring him to the store with you and let him choose between two bed choices.

In addition, let him pick out special sheets for his bed. Getting him involved in the process will get him more excited and interested in making the switch to a big bed. Finally, you may want to have a special get together where your child invites a few special friends or family members for a "big bed party." Make them proud of their new transition.

My baby throws her blanket (stuffed animal) out of bed. Should I go back in to retrieve it?

If you see or suspect that your baby has thrown or accidentally dropped her blanket or stuffed animal out of her bed, it is okay to go in once to return it to her. However, if she continues to throw it over do not repeatedly go in to return it to her. As hard as this sounds, it will only make things worse because your child is now turning this into a game to stall bedtime. Eventually she will learn that she should not throw it over the rail.

My child is two years old. Is my child too old to sleep coach?

It is never too late to start sleep coaching your childGood sleep habits are a learned skill that you must teach your child. It may take a little longer and be a little more difficult because your child has had a longer time period to develop bad sleep habits. However, if you are consistent both you and your child will be happier in the end.

Can I still sleep coach my child if he is adopted?

If you adopted your child as a newborn, there is no reason why you would need to do anything different when deciding to sleep coach your baby. If you adopted your child at an older age, then you should spend the first few months getting to know and bond with your baby before starting the sleep coaching process.

My baby was born four weeks premature. When can I start sleep coaching my child?

If your baby was born prematurely then you need to adjust your child's age to that of their gestational age. So if your child was born four weeks premature, your child will need to be five months (four months plus four weeks).

Can I still sleep coach my child if he has been diagnosed with reflux?

In most cases, it is still possible to sleep coach your baby even if he has been diagnosed with reflux as long as your baby is not experiencing pain. Only in extreme cases, sleep coaching with reflux may need to be delayed. As with any other medical condition, check with your pediatrician first.

Some solutions for babies with reflux are to burp baby frequently, feed small amounts in shorter intervals, have baby sleep on an incline, and keep baby upright while awake. You can purchase a wedge to use as an incline under your baby's sheet at any baby store, purchase baby bed blocks or you can place books under the crib legs on the side in which your baby sleeps. Minimize time spent in the car seat because this position is actually worse for the reflux.

Can I still sleep coach my baby if he is sharing a room with his sibling?

Yes, it is possible to sleep train your baby if he shares a room with either you or a sibling. However, during the sleep coaching process, you need to relocate the sibling (or yourselves) temporarily until you have successfully sleep coached the baby. You can have your older child sleep in your room for a few nights. As parents, you can try sleeping in the living room or another temporary room in the house during the process.

How come my baby seems more tired now that he is getting more sleep?

This comes down to the old adage, "sleep begets sleep." Also as your baby's sleep improves, his body craves more sleep to "catch up" on all the sleep he has lost. Once, he is all caught up, he will not appear as tired.

When is the best day to start sleep coaching?

I highly recommend to start sleep coaching your child on a weekend. This way you do not have to worry about work or other obligations when you are most likely going to be a little more tired than usual. You will also have more time to devote to the sleep coaching process.

How long will it take before I see results?

Depending on which method you have chosen to sleep coach your baby, you may begin to see results anywhere from three days to two weeks. The less crying involved during the process the longer it will most likely take. As long as you are consistent and stick with your method both you and your baby will be happier in the end.

What do I do if my baby makes himself throw up during the sleep coaching process?

If your baby purposefully vomits or vomits from crying during the sleep coaching process, go into his room clean him up and change his bed. It is also possible to layer your baby's crib with a mattress cover and sheets so that you can just peel off the top layer for a quicker change. Do so with minimal to no interaction. If you interact with baby, he will perceive it as a game or a way to get attention and may continue to vomit. Your baby will learn to stop this behavior.

How do I continue my sleep coaching progress if my child is in daycare?

Make sure that the daycare provider is aware of your sleep coaching plan and that you are on the same page. Speak with them ahead of time to see if they are able to accommodate this change. If not, try and take off some time from work (i.e four days or two days before or after a weekend) to help your baby nap during the day and return her to daycare when her napping has improved. Lastly, see if your daycare provider would be willing to use a noise machine during nap time to help filter out any outside noises. (It would be a benefit for all the babies.)

Bumps in the Road

*My baby is suffering from colic. Is there
anything I can do to help him sleep?*

The technical definition of colic is "crying
lasting for three or more hours per day for more than
three days a week for longer than three weeks. In
most cases, colic begins within the first three weeks of
life and can continue up to twelve weeks or longer.
Colic is not a sleep problem. However, colicky infants
appear to have a shorter duration of total sleep.

Some theorize that colic results from
overstimulation. The baby cannot handle the world
around him and therefore cries to shut it out. Sleep
deprivation (when your baby does not get the proper
sleep) may contribute to colic.

Sleep problems may often persist after the
infant has outgrown colic because the strategies
developed to decrease the crying spells (i.e. rocking,
frequent holding, etc.) often interfere with the
development of normal sleep patterns.

There are some methods you can try to soothe
a colicky baby. First of all, do not overfeed your baby.
Stick to your baby's regular feeding schedule of
timing and amount. In addition, try walking the baby
in a front pouch style carrier. You can also draw
baby's legs up to decrease pressure off his belly.

Swaddle your baby. Soothe your baby with
rhythmic steady movements (like rocking gently) or

with sounds (like white noise or running a vacuum). Only employ these methods when completely necessary and be prepared to wean your baby from them as soon as the colic passes.

My baby still wakes up very early even though he is going to bed with no problem?

Between approximately four to six in the morning, your baby enters a light sleep state. He will then again go into the very deep sleep one last time before rising for the day (about thirty minutes to an hour prior to waking up). Any waking before six in the morning needs to be treated as a night waking. Use your sleep coaching method during the time to get your baby back to sleep.

What do I do if my baby wakes up after only thirty to forty minutes into a nap?

It is very common for a baby to take a twenty to forty five minute nap. Many babies when they are overtired or who do not fall asleep on their own only nap for a short period of time. What happens is at the end of a sleep cycle (which is roughly thirty to forty minutes) your baby will come into a lighter stage of sleep. At this point, you want her to continue on to the next cycle of sleep. However, if she fell asleep in your arms, then she will most likely wake up in the crib, start crying and not be able to soothe herself back to sleep wondering where you've gone. Make sure you are putting your baby down drowsy but awake. Once he has mastered putting himself to sleep, he should start sleeping longer than thirty minutes.

If your baby is a chronic short napper, then it is going to take time for her to train her body to start sleeping longer for nap time. Your baby may be soothing herself to sleep but still waking after only thirty to forty minutes. If this is the case, as soon as your baby starts to cry (a little more than a stir), go in and try to soothe her back to sleep to try to lengthen the nap. You can try using a gentle touch, some shushing, patting her back, or bouncing the mattress lightly. If this backfires (your baby becomes agitated and more awake, then take her out.)

Next time she awakens early from a nap, try and let her cry for a few minutes to see if she will fall back to sleep on her own. However, most parents find that once their baby learns to soothe themselves to sleep and his night time sleep is fixed, then the daytime naps lengthen and fall into place, as well. If you're child appears well rested and well behaved after forty minute naps, and a full night's sleep, this may be all she needs (although this is often not true.)

Whatever the case, it will be much better if you can salvage the nap so that she has a fairly solid nap. If the soothing back to sleep or letting her cry has not worked after ten or fifteen minutes of trying, then it is probably not going to because she has had just enough sleep to be alert, although not enough sleep to be considered restorative.

The longer a baby has slept the less likely she is to fall back asleep when waking from a nap. Try to keep your baby up to the next scheduled nap time. If she cannot quite make it to the next nap time, then you can put her in a little earlier. If your baby naps when she should be awake, it throws the remaining sleep/wake schedule off track.

It is a bit of work but you can definitely get her sleeping longer than twenty minutes. A nap is considered to be restorative if it is about an hour or longer. Most babies in this age range (five to twelve months) sleep at least a solid hour, although forty to forty five minutes is sometimes enough. Anything shorter than thirty minutes should be considered a nap. As your baby begins to nap longer, you will find that she will be much happier when she is awake.

My baby is sick. How do I help comfort him without creating any negative sleep habits?

Medical factors can interfere with infant sleep and, if persistent lead to sleep disturbance. Ear infections, common colds, and teething can all cause temporary discomfort and disrupt sleep in some infants. If these conditions recur frequently or if the parental response to the disturbance differs from the normal routine, disruption may lead to a more fixed pattern of nightly awakenings.

When your child is sick, respond immediately to their nighttime crying. Do whatever you need to soothe and comfort him, whether it be changing his diaper, giving him medicine, suctioning his nose, or rocking him.

Once, the illness is over, expect your child to wake up during the night. At this point, continue with or go back to the sleep coaching technique that you previously utilized. It is important to get your baby back on track as soon as possible and do not let new habits develop. You do not want to undo all that you have already accomplished.

We are planning a vacation with our baby. How do we continue to keep our baby sleeping well and not mess up everything we have worked so hard to achieve?

When you travel, it is okay to alter your baby's sleep routine but I would not recommend altering it drastically. Yes, you spend a lot of money to take a vacation but at the same time, you want to be able to enjoy it. You do not want to be dealing with an overly sleep deprived baby.

First, pack some familiar items from home so that your child will feel comfortable and secure in his new environment (i.e. a favorite stuffed animal/blanket, book, etc.) I would also recommend making sure that your baby will have his own bed to sleep in (pack-n-play, port-a-crib, etc.). Now is not the time to instill the family bed, or place your baby in an unsafe place to sleep. In addition, I recommend bringing along a sound machine (if you are using it at home) and a night-light if necessary.

As for the sleep routine during vacation, try and go back to the hotel or place you are staying at for at least one of your baby's naps. This will allow for a much needed rest for both you and your baby. This way your baby can sleep in an undisturbed environment and will be refreshed for the second half of the day. At bedtime, it is okay to put the baby to bed within one to two hours of their normal bedtime depending on their age. Follow a similar routine as you would at home when putting your baby to sleep. If you have to be in the same room with the baby upon his or her falling asleep, keep the lights dim, noise level down, and avoid eye contact. Remember this may not sound fun, however it will make for a better vacation because your baby will be happier and more cooperative when he is awake.

We are invited to a birthday party that is right in the middle of my baby's nap. What can I do?

There will be times when the need arises to alter your baby's routine for special events or holidays (i.e. Thanksgiving, first birthday, etc.). Because this event usually takes place for one day, it should not have too much of an impact on your baby's sleep routine. Do whatever it takes to accommodate the special occasion.

If you can, plan the event around a nap. For example, for your baby's first birthday, if you know that she naps from one to three p.m., have the party in the morning or after her nap so that she will be cheerful for the party. Nothing is worse than having the star of the show cranky or asleep during her own party.

If you know you have to travel to a relative's house for a holiday and will be returning late, pack a nighttime diaper and pajamas so that you can get your baby ready before you leave. Then if your baby falls asleep in the car on the way home, all you have to do is transfer him to his bed. Make sure that you have no major plans the day after a special occasion so that both you and your baby will have a chance to rest and catch up on some much needed sleep from the day before. Your baby will most likely be more tired the next day and require a longer nap time.

How do I adjust my baby's schedule when we change the clocks for daylight savings time?

Just when you have a routine established, daylight savings time comes along and threatens to wreak havoc. It does not have to be as bad as it sounds. When it is time to change the clocks, if it is "spring ahead" (moving the clocks forward), place your baby in bed at the same time as you did before according to the new time.

For example, if your child goes to sleep at seven thirty and you move the clocks forward so that seven thirty new time is really six thirty old time, continue to put your child to bed at seven thirty new time. This will not be a problem and may actually help catch them up on any much-needed sleep.

However, if you are "falling back" (setting the clocks backward), place your baby to bed ten minutes earlier each night the week before the anticipated time change. For example, if your baby normally goes to bed around seven thirty, start by putting her to bed seven twenty seven days before the time change, then seven ten, six days before the time change, etc.

This will allow for her body to adjust to the new time. If you do not do this you may have a hard time initially with the time change because your baby may not be able to stay up to her usual bedtime. If you forget to adjust the bedtime a week before you turn the clocks backward, you can put your baby to bed one hour earlier than normal on the day you turn the clocks backward so that she does not get overtired and cranky.

We are traveling to another time zone. Is there any way I can ease my baby's adjustment to the new time either before we leave or when we arrive?

In anticipation of the trip, put your child to bed fifteen minutes earlier/later (depending on the time zone) each night than his normal bedtime. Gradually increase the fifteen-minute increments each night for the week before your trip. By the time you are set to leave for your destination, your child will be better able to adapt to the new time zone.

If when you arrive at your destination, your child is irritable and tired, let him sleep when he wants to sleep. It is better to deal with an off schedule child than an overtired child. If you are traveling to a time zone that is behind yours, it is also very helpful to bring your child outside to a play as soon as you get there if it is still daylight. This will help his body adjust faster to the new time zone.

Do I use the same sleep coaching method that I use at night to get my baby to nap?

You need to use the same sleep coaching method whenever you put your baby to sleep. You need to be consistent and this way your baby will also know what to expect and therefore learn faster. So whatever method you use, use it at nap time and bed time.

There is only one difference. At nap time if your baby is still awake after an hour of being placed in his bed and shows no signs of going to sleep, pick him up, praise him for trying and take him out. If your baby is younger than six months of age you will want to try to put him in for a nap again within one to two hours. If your baby is older than six months, you want to try again at his next nap time (the time he would normally take his next nap).

Also, refrain from taking him in the stroller, car trip, or anything else that my lull him to sleep. Remember you need to teach him how to fall asleep on his own. The only time you may need to help him get to sleep is if he has not napped all day. At this point, do whatever it takes to get him to take a nap so it will make it easier for him to go to sleep that night. Just make sure that the nap is not too close to his bedtime.

Remember the bedtime routine can also be used before a nap time. It is believed that the part of the brain that is responsible for day time sleep is different than that for night time sleep. Therefore, the routine can be shortened for nap time. For example, you can read a story and sing a lullaby before a nap. The familiar activities will relax your child and give her cue that it is time to go to sleep.

Suggested Bedtime Routines

- Bathing or washing hands/face
- Putting on pajamas
- Reading a story
- Wiping baby's gums/Brushing teeth
- Talking with your baby
- Saying goodnight to objects around the room
- Singing a lullaby
- Playing some quiet music
- Massage
- Feeding

How do I know when to drop a nap?

As your baby grows you will begin to see signs that it is time for her nap schedule to change. When you baby takes a long time to fall asleep for a nap, suddenly starts taking a very short nap after napping for a longer period, or has trouble falling asleep at night, then it is time to reevaluate her nap schedule.

For example when switching from two naps to one, you may notice that your child has difficulty falling asleep at night because she is waking from her second nap so late. It is then time to shift her to one nap a day and put her to bed earlier at night. Always refer to the "Recommended Hours of Sleep by Age" chart in Appendix C.

15

A Few Last Words of Encouragement

Overall, please remember the most common recommendation to decrease sleep problems is to establish regular routines and by teaching your child to self-soothe. By allowing your child the ability to self soothe to sleep, your child will be able to sleep for longer periods at a time, and be able to put himself back to sleep when he wakes up at night. Remember sleep induces more sleep and makes it easier to fall asleep.

Be consistent! This applies to the routine as well as what method you use to get your child to sleep. Respect your child's need for sleep and help with the process of establishing good sleep patterns. Remember, methods that do not allow for crying or minimal crying can take a week to several weeks to work, so be patient.

It's important to be consistent with a particular method for at least a week before evaluating whether or not the situation is improving. It is easier to create an unpleasant situation than it is to fix one. However, it will likely take another week or more for any method to be fully effective.

Recent research has shown that babies and toddlers are more securely attached and happier after sleep coaching. All children are different and if you follow one of these methods consistently, your child will be quickly on his or her way to developing a healthy sleep routine! In addition, you as parents will be pleased with how much better your life has become. I know you CAN do it!

Happy Sleeping!

Appendix A:
The Baby Sleep Coach's
Daily Journal

This journal will be beneficial in getting your baby to sleep through the night.

To use this journal:

1. Fill out the sleep plans as indicated after reviewing **The Baby Sleep Coach System.**

2. On the daily journal pages, place a check mark and the exact time (where applicable) under the appropriate column next to the corresponding time box. Be sure to mark down the exact wake up time and any night wakings as well. (i.e. your child woke up at 6:14 am, so you write "6:14"). It is also helpful to mark down when each feeding was and the total amount (i.e. minutes nursed or ounces consumed). See the example chart that follows.

My Bedtime Plan

Child's Name:

Date:

My bedtime goal will be _____ o'clock p.m.

We will perform the following routine:

       1.
       2.
       3.
       4.
       5.
       6.

If _____ cries after putting him/ her in bed we will:

If _____ wakes up during the night, we will:

I will not get _____ if he/she awakens before 6 in the morning.

I understand that this bedtime plan will improve my child's sleep habits, help my child sleep through the night and make him/her a happier child during the day. I am willing to be consistent in my methods and carry out my bedtime sleep plan as described above.

Signed:

_____

Signed:

_____

My Nap Time Plan

Child's Name:

Date:

My nap time goal will be _____ naps per day.

_____ has to be in bed _____ hours after his/her morning wake up time and _____ hours after awaking from his/her morning nap.

We will perform the following routine:

        1.
        2.
        3.

If _____ cries after putting him/her in bed we will:

If _____ wakes up after sleeping less than 30 minutes, we willI understand that this nap time plan will improve my child's sleep habits, help him/her sleep through the night and make him/her a happier child during the day. I am willing to be consistent in my methods and carry out my nap time sleep plan as described above.

Signed:

_____

Signed:

_____

The Baby Sleep Coach's Daily Journal

Date:

	Feeding	Sleeping	Awake	Fussy
6 a.m.				
7 a.m.				
8 a.m.				
9 a.m.				
10 a.m.				
11 a.m.				
12 p.m.				
1 p.m.				
2 p.m.				
3 p.m.				
4 p.m.				
5 p.m.				
6 p.m.				
7 p.m.				
8 p.m.				
9 p.m.				
10 p.m.				
11 p.m.				
12 a.m.				
1 a.m.				
2 a.m.				
3 a.m.				
4 a.m.				
5 a.m.				

The Baby Sleep Coach's Daily Journal

Date:

	Feeding	Sleeping	Awake	Fussy
6 a.m.				
7 a.m.				
8 a.m.				
9 a.m.				
10 a.m.				
11 a.m.				
12 p.m.				
1 p.m.				
2 p.m.				
3 p.m.				
4 p.m.				
5 p.m.				
6 p.m.				
7 p.m.				
8 p.m.				
9 p.m.				
10 p.m.				
11 p.m.				
12 a.m.				
1 a.m.				
2 a.m.				
3 a.m.				
4 a.m.				
5 a.m.				

The Baby Sleep Coach's Daily Journal
Date:

	Feeding	Sleeping	Awake	Fussy
6 a.m.				
7 a.m.				
8 a.m.				
9 a.m.				
10 a.m.				
11 a.m.				
12 p.m.				
1 p.m.				
2 p.m.				
3 p.m.				
4 p.m.				
5 p.m.				
6 p.m.				
7 p.m.				
8 p.m.				
9 p.m.				
10 p.m.				
11 p.m.				
12 a.m.				
1 a.m.				
2 a.m.				
3 a.m.				
4 a.m.				
5 a.m.				

The Baby Sleep Coach's Daily Journal

Date:

	Feeding	Sleeping	Awake	Fussy
6 a.m.				
7 a.m.				
8 a.m.				
9 a.m.				
10 a.m.				
11 a.m.				
12 p.m.				
1 p.m.				
2 p.m.				
3 p.m.				
4 p.m.				
5 p.m.				
6 p.m.				
7 p.m.				
8 p.m.				
9 p.m.				
10 p.m.				
11 p.m.				
12 a.m.				
1 a.m.				
2 a.m.				
3 a.m.				
4 a.m.				
5 a.m.				

The Baby Sleep Coach's Daily Journal
Date:

	Feeding	Sleeping	Awake	Fussy
6 a.m.				
7 a.m.				
8 a.m.				
9 a.m.				
10 a.m.				
11 a.m.				
12 p.m.				
1 p.m.				
2 p.m.				
3 p.m.				
4 p.m.				
5 p.m.				
6 p.m.				
7 p.m.				
8 p.m.				
9 p.m.				
10 p.m.				
11 p.m.				
12 a.m.				
1 a.m.				
2 a.m.				
3 a.m.				
4 a.m.				
5 a.m.				

The Baby Sleep Coach's Daily Journal

Date:

	Feeding	Sleeping	Awake	Fussy
6 a.m.				
7 a.m.				
8 a.m.				
9 a.m.				
10 a.m.				
11 a.m.				
12 p.m.				
1 p.m.				
2 p.m.				
3 p.m.				
4 p.m.				
5 p.m.				
6 p.m.				
7 p.m.				
8 p.m.				
9 p.m.				
10 p.m.				
11 p.m.				
12 a.m.				
1 a.m.				
2 a.m.				
3 a.m.				
4 a.m.				
5 a.m.				

The Baby Sleep Coach's Daily Journal

Date:

	Feeding	Sleeping	Awake	Fussy
6 a.m.				
7 a.m.				
8 a.m.				
9 a.m.				
10 a.m.				
11 a.m.				
12 p.m.				
1 p.m.				
2 p.m.				
3 p.m.				
4 p.m.				
5 p.m.				
6 p.m.				
7 p.m.				
8 p.m.				
9 p.m.				
10 p.m.				
11 p.m.				
12 a.m.				
1 a.m.				
2 a.m.				
3 a.m.				
4 a.m.				
5 a.m.				

The Baby Sleep Coach's Daily Journal

Date:

	Feeding	Sleeping	Awake	Fussy
6 a.m.				
7 a.m.				
8 a.m.				
9 a.m.				
10 a.m.				
11 a.m.				
12 p.m.				
1 p.m.				
2 p.m.				
3 p.m.				
4 p.m.				
5 p.m.				
6 p.m.				
7 p.m.				
8 p.m.				
9 p.m.				
10 p.m.				
11 p.m.				
12 a.m.				
1 a.m.				
2 a.m.				
3 a.m.				
4 a.m.				
5 a.m.				

The Baby Sleep Coach's Daily Journal

Date:

	Feeding	Sleeping	Awake	Fussy
6 a.m.				
7 a.m.				
8 a.m.				
9 a.m.				
10 a.m.				
11 a.m.				
12 p.m.				
1 p.m.				
2 p.m.				
3 p.m.				
4 p.m.				
5 p.m.				
6 p.m.				
7 p.m.				
8 p.m.				
9 p.m.				
10 p.m.				
11 p.m.				
12 a.m.				
1 a.m.				
2 a.m.				
3 a.m.				
4 a.m.				
5 a.m.				

The Baby Sleep Coach's Daily Journal

Date:

	Feeding	Sleeping	Awake	Fussy
6 a.m.				
7 a.m.				
8 a.m.				
9 a.m.				
10 a.m.				
11 a.m.				
12 p.m.				
1 p.m.				
2 p.m.				
3 p.m.				
4 p.m.				
5 p.m.				
6 p.m.				
7 p.m.				
8 p.m.				
9 p.m.				
10 p.m.				
11 p.m.				
12 a.m.				
1 a.m.				
2 a.m.				
3 a.m.				
4 a.m.				
5 a.m.				

The Baby Sleep Coach's Daily Journal

Date:

	Feeding	Sleeping	Awake	Fussy
6 a.m.				
7 a.m.				
8 a.m.				
9 a.m.				
10 a.m.				
11 a.m.				
12 p.m.				
1 p.m.				
2 p.m.				
3 p.m.				
4 p.m.				
5 p.m.				
6 p.m.				
7 p.m.				
8 p.m.				
9 p.m.				
10 p.m.				
11 p.m.				
12 a.m.				
1 a.m.				
2 a.m.				
3 a.m.				
4 a.m.				
5 a.m.				

The Baby Sleep Coach's Daily Journal

Date:

	Feeding	Sleeping	Awake	Fussy
6 a.m.				
7 a.m.				
8 a.m.				
9 a.m.				
10 a.m.				
11 a.m.				
12 p.m.				
1 p.m.				
2 p.m.				
3 p.m.				
4 p.m.				
5 p.m.				
6 p.m.				
7 p.m.				
8 p.m.				
9 p.m.				
10 p.m.				
11 p.m.				
12 a.m.				
1 a.m.				
2 a.m.				
3 a.m.				
4 a.m.				
5 a.m.				

The Baby Sleep Coach's Daily Journal

Date:

	Feeding	Sleeping	Awake	Fussy
6 a.m.				
7 a.m.				
8 a.m.				
9 a.m.				
10 a.m.				
11 a.m.				
12 p.m.				
1 p.m.				
2 p.m.				
3 p.m.				
4 p.m.				
5 p.m.				
6 p.m.				
7 p.m.				
8 p.m.				
9 p.m.				
10 p.m.				
11 p.m.				
12 a.m.				
1 a.m.				
2 a.m.				
3 a.m.				
4 a.m.				
5 a.m.				

The Baby Sleep Coach's Daily Journal

Date:

	Feeding	Sleeping	Awake	Fussy
6 a.m.				
7 a.m.				
8 a.m.				
9 a.m.				
10 a.m.				
11 a.m.				
12 p.m.				
1 p.m.				
2 p.m.				
3 p.m.				
4 p.m.				
5 p.m.				
6 p.m.				
7 p.m.				
8 p.m.				
9 p.m.				
10 p.m.				
11 p.m.				
12 a.m.				
1 a.m.				
2 a.m.				
3 a.m.				
4 a.m.				
5 a.m.				

Appendix B:
The Baby Sleep Coach's
Plan & Chart Examples

My Bedtime Plan

Child's Name: Taylor

Date: 8/26/07

My bedtime goal will be _7_ o'clock p.m.

We will perform the following routine:

1. bath
2. Put PJs on
3. Bottle
4. Brush teeth
5. Read books
6. Say goodnight

If <u>Taylor</u> cries after putting him/her in bed
we will:
<u>briefly check in on her after 5 minutes. If
she continues to cry we will briefly check in
on her after 10 minutes. If she continues to
cry, we will briefly check on her after 15
minutes.</u>

If <u>Taylor</u> wakes up during the night, we will:
<u>Wait to see if she is really awake. If she is we
will briefly check on her in 15 minute intervals
until she goes back to sleep.</u>

I will not get <u>Taylor</u> out of bed if he/she
awakens before 6 in the morning.

I understand that this bedtime plan will
improve my child's sleep habits, help my
child sleep through the night and make him/
her a happier child during the day. I am
willing to be consistent in my methods and
carry out my bedtime sleep plan as
described above.

Signed: **<u>Taylor's Mom</u>**

Signed: **<u>Taylor's Dad</u>**

My Nap Time Plan

Child's Name: Taylor

Date: 8/26/07

My nap time goal will be 2 **naps per day.**

<u>Taylor</u> **has to be in bed** 2 **hours after his/her morning wake up time and** 2 ½ **hours after awaking from his/her morning nap.**

We will perform the following routine:

1. change diaper
2. read books
3. say goodnight

If <u>Taylor</u> **cries after putting him/her in bed we will:**

<u>Check in on her briefly after 15 minute intervals. If she has not fallen asleep after 1</u>

hour, we will take her out of her bed and wait for her next nap time.

If Taylor wakes up after sleeping less than 30 minutes, we will:
we will wait to make sure that Taylor is just not stirring. We will then go in comfort her back to sleep to try and extend her nap.

I understand that this nap time plan will improve my child's sleep habits, help him/ her sleep through the night and make him/ her a happier child during the day. I am willing to be consistent in my methods and carry out my nap time sleep plan as described above.

Signed: Taylor's Mom

Signed: Taylor's Dad

The Baby Sleep Coach's Daily Journal
Date: 8/26

	Feeding	Sleeping	Awake	Fussy
6 a.m.			√ 6:14	
7 a.m.	√ 5 oz.		√	
8 a.m.		√ 8:05		
9 a.m.		√		
10 a.m.			√ 10:11	
11 a.m.	√ 5 oz		√	
12 p.m.		√ 12:35		
1 p.m.		√		
2 p.m.			√ 2:40	
3 p.m.	√ 5 oz.		√	
4 p.m.		√ 4:01	√ 4:50	
5 p.m.			√	
6 p.m.			√	√
7 p.m.	√ 6 oz.	√ 7:45		
8 p.m.		√		
9 p.m.		√		
10 p.m.		√		
11 p.m.	√ 5 oz.	√		
12 a.m.		√		
1 a.m.		√		
2 a.m.		√		
3 a.m.		√		
4 a.m.		√		
5 a.m.		√		

Appendix C:
An Overview of Recommended
Hours of Sleep by Age

Age	Nighttime Sleep	Naps*
Newborn	9 hours	8 hours (sporadic)
One month	8 hours	8 hours (sporadic)
Three months	10 hours	5 hours (3)
Six months	11 hours	3 1/2 hours (2)
Nine months	11 hours	3 hours (2)
Fifteen months	11 ¼ hours	2-3 hours (1-2)
Two years old	11 hours	2 hours (1)
Four years old	11 ½ hours	No nap
Five years old	11 hours	No nap

*Number of naps is in parentheses

Appendix D:
Overview of Recommended Windows of Wakefulness for Naps by Age

Age	To First Nap	To Second Nap	To Third Nap
0-3 mos.:	No more than 1 to 2 hours of wakefulness		
3-4 mos.:	1 to 2 hours	2 hours	2 hours
4-6 mos.:	2 hours	2 ½ hours	2 ½ hours
6-9 mos.:	2 ½ hours	3 hours	N/A
9 -12 mos.:	3 hours	3 ½ hours	N/A
12-18 mos.:	3 ½ hours	3 ½ to 4 hours	N/A
18–24 mos.:	4-5 hours	N/A	N/A
2 yrs.:	6 hours	N/A	N/A
3 – 5 yrs.:	7 hours	N/A	N/A

Index

checking in,

  after vomiting, 171

  early waking, 163, 173

climbing out of crib, 81, 154-55,

    165-66

clock, 136

cluster feeding, 67

colic, 43, 172-173

cosleeping,

  safe sleeping and, 81, 123

crib,

  moving to bed, 81, 154, 156

  toys, 43-44, 81, 85, 151

crying,

  after sleep coaching, 166

  deciphering, 32-34

  types, 33

  vomiting, 171

  why, 38

D

daily journal, 190-203, 209

daycare, 171

daylight savings time, 178-79

day/night reversal, 150

developmental milestones,

  rolling over, 150

  separation anxiety, 152

  standing in crib, 151

  starting solids, 153-54

diapers, nighttime, 60, 85, 126,

    163

dream feeding, 65

E

early morning riser, 163, 173

eating/sleeping

  connection, 27-31

excessive sleepiness, 170

extinction burst, 164-65

F

falling asleep, 40, 80, 103,118

  during feeding, 31, 76

F.A.S.T plan, 60-64

feedings,

  average time, 31-32

  keeping baby awake, 27

  sleep and, 27-31

  transfer to day, 87-89

fussiness, calming, 47-51

V

W

Have Some Questions?
Need More Help?

Go now to:

www.babysleepcoach.com

and click on the private sleep coaching tab to
see the **follow up support services** that
accompany this book. The package includes:

- **A private, 45-minute consultation by phone**
  where specific questions and issues that
  have arisen in the sleep coaching process
  will be addressed.

- **One follow-up email session** where you
  can email me with any additional questions
  that you might have after our phone
  consultation.

or email me for more information at:

drheather@babysleepcoach.com